CW00404723

Sustaining the Compreh

Trevor Male · Ioanna Palaiologou

Sustaining the Comprehensive Ideal

The Robert Clack School

Trevor Male
Institute of Education
University College London
London, UK

Ioanna Palaiologou
Institute of Education
University College London
London, UK

ISBN 978-3-030-34158-9   ISBN 978-3-030-34156-5   (eBook)
https://doi.org/10.1007/978-3-030-34156-5

This Palgrave Pivot imprint is published by the registered company Springer Nature Switzerland AG
The registered company address is: Gewerbestrasse 11, 6330 Cham, Switzerland

CONTENTS

LIST OF TABLES

CHAPTER 1

Introduction

Abstract This chapter provides the background information for the story of the Robert Clack School, a state-funded secondary school in England in the London Borough of Barking and Dagenham, which went from being a well-respected school to one that was in a state of abject failure in the mid-1990s. The chapter initially details the history of the outer London borough which has experienced radical changes to the local population and economy in the current century. Throughout this time, the borough has experienced sustained high levels of poverty with a decline in the local manufacturing industry (notably the Ford Motor Company) and despite radical changes in the age and ethnicity of the local population. The local education authority (LEA) was committed to the notion of equal opportunity for all students and subscribed to the 'comprehensive ideal', the education of all local children in a single school. During the 1990s, however, the Robert Clack Comprehensive School (as it was named at the time) was exhibiting chronic levels of underperformance, highlighted in an inspection report of 1995, which ultimately led to a change in school leadership in 1997. The appointment of a new headteacher was surprising as the successful candidate, Paul Grant, was a radical choice as a head of department within the school with no previous senior leadership experience.

Keywords Secondary education · Comprehensive ideal · Working-class · Critical hope · Improvement

© The Author(s) 2019
T. Male and I. Palaiologou, *Sustaining the Comprehensive Ideal*,
https://doi.org/10.1007/978-3-030-34156-5_1

1

THE STORY BEGINS

This book tells the story of the Robert Clack School, a state-maintained comprehensive secondary school in England, and analyses how the school made the transition from failure to success and has managed to sustain and enhance that status over a period of 20 years (1997–2017) despite changes in local demographics which resulted in the school serving a significantly different ethnic community than was evident at the start of their journey of improvement.

The school is situated in the Becontree Estate in the London Borough of Barking and Dagenham, an area of in the extreme east of England's capital city that has consistently featured as one of poverty. Unlike some other schools which changed their student population in search of success, the school continues to serve its immediate local community which comprises almost mainly working-class families. It is remarkable story of success based on a desire to confront disadvantage, particularly by the headteacher throughout this period. This approach bears resemblance to the concept of *critical hope* (Duncan-Andrade 2009) where the needs of young people in disadvantaged communities are recognised and addressed in order to provide them with 'control of destiny' whereby they learn 'to deal with the forces that affect their lives, even if they decide not to deal with them' (Syme 2004: 3).

The findings provided in this book are primarily based on data the authors collected from site-based interviews between 2012 and 2016 in the school with the headteacher, other senior leaders, governors, teaching staff, support staff, students, local authority officers and parents. The data set also includes reviews of secondary documentation such as Ofsted reports, internal documentation, press cuttings and correspondence between a parent governor and the previous headteacher. All interviews were audio recorded, professionally transcribed and subsequently analysed through a process of open coding, supplemented by axial coding into the thematic analysis which shapes the book.

Our analysis demonstrates that the ethos underpinning the school's sustained improvement is a desire to meet the needs of young people in disadvantaged communities in a quest to allow them to transcend their situation. The consequence of the sustained effort we have seen is that that the school has exceeded its prescribed expectations, continues to improve and has lifted both the students and the community's aspirations exponentially (Palaiologou and Male 2016). This is a school, we conclude, that epitomises the 'comprehensive ideal' of secondary education in England, a simple premise that affirms that children's education should not be disadvantaged by their backgrounds and that the state should provide free, high-quality education for all (Pring and Walford 1997: 6).

THE COMPREHENSIVE IDEAL

The ideas and principles that underpin the notion of comprehensive schools seemed to first emerge in 1918 when a committee of the American teachers' union, the National Education Association, met to consider the future character of the high school curriculum. Their report, 'Cardinal Principles of Secondary Education', rejected a class-based system and instead argued for an approach to secondary schooling that included provisions for 'unifying youths with different backgrounds, abilities, and aspirations so that they would learn to live together in a diverse democratic society' (Wraga 1999: 296). The pioneers of comprehensive education placed 'new faith in human educability which took the place of the fatalism of the past [and to offer] a full, all-round education for all' (Simon 1997: 26). In its purest form, 'education should be accessible to all pupils regardless of capacity or background, and "worthwhileness", in that the curriculum has to be of defensible value so that it enhances the future lives of its students' (Holt 1999: 330).

The notion of comprehensive schools as an alternative to the organisation of secondary education in England, Wales and Northern Ireland grew in the period after the Second World War of 1939–1945 due mainly to the determination of socialist political figures to move towards the concept of meritocracy in a society that stubbornly continued to favour a privileged few. At the forefront in this debate was the selection process, known as the Eleven Plus (11+), that led to a small proportion of children going to on to grammar schools for their secondary education whilst a few went to secondary technical schools, with the vast majority consigned to Secondary modern schools. This was the tripartite system of secondary education that was identified in the 1944 Education Act and 1947 Education (Northern Ireland) Act. The ambition of the tripartite system was for children to be provided with the type of education which most suited their needs and abilities and was underpinned by the principle that 'the nature of a child's education should be based on his capacity and promise and not by the circumstances of his parent' (Board of Education 1943: 7).

A school system was thus envisaged in which skill was to be the major factor in deciding access to education, rather than financial resources, and one that would meet the needs of the economy, providing intellectuals, technicians and general workers with an education appropriate to their field of employment. Prior to this time, state-funded secondary education had been poorly organised through a combination of local government, private charities and religious foundations. Grammar schools had been perceived as the route to ensure the future success of the brightest state-funded pupils and had been populated mainly by privileged children, typically from middle-class families. The post-war legislation sought to provide universal basic secondary education that raised the age of leaving school from 14 to 15 years (later extended to 16 in 1972).

Each category of state-run secondary schools was designed with a specific purpose in mind, aiming to impart a range of skills appropriate to the needs and future careers of their pupils.

- *Grammar schools* were intended to teach a highly academic curriculum, with a strong focus on intellectual subjects;
- *Secondary technical schools* were designed to train children adept in mechanical and scientific subjects. The focus of the schools was on providing high academic standards in demanding subjects such as physics, chemistry, advanced mathematics and biology to create pupils that could become scientists, engineers and technicians;
- *Secondary modern schools* would train pupils in practical skills, aimed at equipping them for less-skilled jobs and home management.

The Robert Clack School was named after the two-time Mayor of Dagenham who served from 1940–1942, but died suddenly at the age of 51 years in 1953. Robert Clack was known as a fighter for social justice, someone who cared passionately about the people of Dagenham and worked tirelessly to secure better outcomes for them. The new school was opened as a secondary technical school in 1955 and was perceived at the time to have relatively high status due to its designation, with parents seemingly preferring a secondary technical school to a secondary modern. In some respects, such a view probably emanates from the way in which secondary moderns were established in the post-war period with no expectation of an examination curriculum, for example, which led to the notion that children either 'passed' the 11+ and went to the grammar school or 'failed' it and went to the local secondary modern.

With local government being put off opening technical schools due to their cost, however, only four per cent of children were attending such schools by 1958. The state school system was effectively a bipartite one, therefore, with grammar schools taking the 'top' 20% or so of children and secondary modern schools taking the rest. In the absence of opportunity for most children to progress the desire for the comprehensivisation of secondary education became a political objective, particularly for those with leanings towards socialist ideals. Grammar schools were seen as divisive and the province of the middle classes, with senior figures in the Labour party setting themselves the goal of removing them from the state system of secondary education. When Antony Crosland became Labour Secretary of State for Education in January 1965, he is alleged (by his wife and biographer) to have said: 'If it's the last thing I do, I'm going to destroy every last [expletive deleted] grammar school' (Crosland 1982: 8), although some close associates have doubted that the quotation is genuine (Reynolds 2005). Irrespective of the colourful language that may have been used, the newly elected Labour government that Crosland served was firmly committed to eliminate separatism in secondary education and issued the infamous Circular 10/65 (Department of Education and Science 1965) which signalled the expectations that the 11+ examination was to be abolished and that local education authorities (LEAs) were to prepare plans to deliver secondary education in their areas on comprehensive lines.

Experiments with comprehensive schools in England and Wales have begun earlier than this in the late 1940s with some LEAs having banished tripartite secondary education in the 1950s. Comprehensive schools were developed because 'there were many who believed that educating all local children in a single school, where they would have equal physical facilities and equal access to high-quality teachers, would raise the aspirations of all children and teachers, bringing about greater equity within the schools and lead to greater opportunities outside in the world of work' (Pring and Walford 1997: 2). By 1970, 115 LEAs had had their reorganisation plans approved, whilst 13 had had theirs rejected, and a further 10 had defied the government and refused to submit any plans at all. The implementation of comprehensive schools was delayed, therefore, not universal and in some instances resisted to the point where even today there are some areas where grammar schools continue to exist.

The Emergence of Barking and Dagenham as a Local Education Authority

The borough was formed in 1965 by the London Government Act 1963 as the London Borough of Barking. The new borough, one of 20 formed as part of Greater London, comprised the Borough of Barking and its predecessors (1882–1965) and the Borough of Dagenham and its predecessors (1926–1965). The name of the borough was later amended by the Local Government Act of 1972 to become the London Borough of Barking and Dagenham.

Like all other boroughs in Greater London, it was to run its maintained schools and associated services through the council's education department, making it a Local Education Authority (LEA). The council has been predominately socialist throughout is existence, represented by the Labour party, with strong inclinations towards supporting comprehensive education that has often brought it into conflict with national Conservative governments seemingly bent on more divisive approaches to schooling. Attainment levels of the borough tended for a long time to be below national averages, and it was repeatedly ranked in the bottom 10% in terms of student attainment according to one of our interviewees, the former Chief Inspector of the LEA (and later Chief Education Officer). This often exposed the borough to attempted repeat interventions in school organisation from external sources and particularly central government agencies. The strength of socialist forces within the council meant, however, the borough was able to resist most intervention attempts or divert them to their own preferred ends. It was not until very recent times that any school in Barking and Dagenham converted to an independent academy, for example, and indeed it took a court injunction on behalf of the Department for Education to impose such a change on one secondary school (see Chapter 5 for more detail).

The council can thus be considered to have enthusiastically embraced the principles of comprehensive education within a local history demonstrating synergy to that policy, with the borough being formed in the same year as the Circular 10/65 and presenting its plans and implementing its plans in advance of the next Labour government to be elected in 1974. Robert Clack Technical School was amalgamated with Triptons Secondary School to form Robert Clack Comprehensive in 1970 (LBBD 2014) and later became a Specialist School for Science in September 2003. The Robert Clack School of Science is now a state-maintained comprehensive school situated in a borough ranked amongst the four lowest in London in 10 of 21 social indicators and one considered to be getting 'slightly worse' according to the data presented by the National Policy Institute (2013).

The Topology and Population of Barking and Dagenham

The borough of Barking and Dagenham has a population of close to 200,000 and is most well known for being the 'home' of the Ford Motor Company in the UK which at one time in the early 1950s employed over 40,000 people. The principal reason for expansion of the borough, however, was the building of a huge council estate (Becontree) in the early 1920s in order to relocate skilled workers from the slums of Inner London after the First World War. Sashin (2011) reports that whilst many people believe that the Becontree Estate was built to accommodate the huge numbers of Ford workers, the development was actually planned well before Ford shifted production to Dagenham from Manchester in 1931. Initially, Ford workers were not allowed to rent property on the estate, but when the London County Council later struggled to keep migrants from the east end of London in their new homes the rules were relaxed to accommodate car workers, a development which started the complementary relationship between the two monolithic cornerstones of the borough's identity—Becontree and Ford. Further, relocation of many Londoners made homeless by the bombing blitz of the Second World War took place when new public housing projects were built in the area.

This history is significant as the population of the borough was almost exclusively white working class at that time and up to the beginning of the current century. Changed circumstances during the latter stages of the previous century led to Ford reducing its output to engines rather than car assembly, however, with a concomitant reduction in job availability (down to just 4000 employees by 2010) which meant the company was no longer the main employer in the area. The population was also an ageing one which, by the new millennium, had the highest proportion of any area in England of people who were 65 or older. As local industry reduced the local economy went into long decline and the area became recognised as one where there was poverty and a need for social welfare, but with a population that was largely white.

This was the situation when the story we tell of the Robert Clack School journey from chronic underperformance and very poor student behaviour begins in 1990. In the following two decades, the astonishing transformation to the school becoming outstanding and excelling 'against the odds' (Ofsted 2009). In terms of attainment in standard examinations, behaviour and student aspirations initially led to it being championed as a leading example of how to support white working-class children. This is not the only way in which the school succeeded, however, as during the same decade the school population changed dramatically and by the national census of 2011 was no longer populated almost entirely by students from white working-class backgrounds.

There were two reasons for the rapid change in the ethnicity of the local population of which social mobility is the major reason, although it also needs to be noted in 1994 local boundaries were change to incorporate the whole of the Becontree estate within Barking and Dagenham. This had the effect of increasing the local population by some 9000, but also meant there was greater diversity of the estate. By far the biggest impact, however, was caused by the economic circumstances of the late 1980s when the Conservative government policy of allowing the purchase of council property was implemented. A local authority planning officer, also a governor of the school, described in his interview how the borough went from having one of the highest proportions of people in their 80s to a much younger population. Many, it appears, took advantage of the housing market by taking the opportunity to sell their former council home (brought at a rate well below the market price) and make a healthy profit before moving out of the area. Consequently, in many instances council tenancy disappeared into the buy-to-let market which means some 25–30% of properties on the local council estate which serves the school are now privately owned leaseholds.

Barking and Dagenham is thus one of the cheapest places to live in London whilst also being served by good transport links to central London through a comprehensive rail transport system. Much of the local immigration into the borough has been driven by economic circumstances as people from other, more expensive areas, recognised the potential of the former council housing stock providing a cheaper place to live. By the time of the 2011 national census, the population describing themselves as White British had declined by some 30% from the previous census of 2001 to just under 50% and the ethnicity of the borough was more in keeping with the rest of London (see Table 1.1). By 2016, the population had grown to 205,000, but was also of significantly lower age with the number of 65+ having reduced to just 13.9 and an average age of 32.9 years with 21% of school age (0–15 years). The changing nature of the ethnicity was startling

Table 1.1 London Borough of Barking and Dagenham 2011 census key statistics

2011 census data Ethnic groups	LBBD % increase/decrease	LBBD % population 2011	LBBD % population 2001	London % population 2011	England % population 2011
White British	−31	49.46	80.86	44.89	79.75
White Other	234	7.81	2.65	12.65	4.58
Mixed/multiple ethnic groups: White and Black Caribbean	88	1.44	0.87	1.46	0.78
Mixed/multiple ethnic groups: White and Black African	272	1.14	0.35	0.80	0.30
Mixed/multiple ethnic groups: White and Asian	133	0.67	0.33	1.24	0.63
Mixed/multiple ethnic groups: Other mixed	234	0.99	0.34	1.45	0.53
Asian/Asian British: Indian	102	4.00	2.25	6.64	2.63
Asian/Asian British: Pakistani	162	4.31	1.86	2.74	2.10
Asian/Asian British: Bangladeshi	1044	4.14	0.41	2.72	0.82
Asian/Asian British: Chinese	70	0.71	0.47	1.52	0.72
Asian/Asian British: Other Asian	485	2.76	0.53	4.88	1.55
Black/African/Caribbean/Black British: African	294	15.43	4.44	7.02	1.84
Black/African/Caribbean/Black British: Caribbean	52	2.81	2.09	4.22	1.11
Black/African/Caribbean/Black British: Other Black	347	1.74	0.44	2.08	0.52
Other ethnic group: Arab		0.52	n/a	1.30	0.42
Other ethnic group: Any other ethnic group	177	1.04	0.43	2.14	0.62

in that 49.5% were now from Black and Minority Ethnic groups and 37.5% had been born abroad (London Data Store 2016).

As may be surmised in the current century, economic migration is not the only reason for increased diversity in the local population, however, as there has also been much immigration of refugees into the country who have located into the area as described by the local authority planning officer and school governor:

> With people coming in from civil war conflicts in Africa and the Balkans people have come here from a wider range of different places, a little rush here, a little rush there. Unlike most of the London boroughs where there tends to be one dominating group from an immigration point, either because they all came at one point or people who came in the first settlement and then other people joined them, here it is a bit more diversified. We have got people from all over the place. Obviously, more recently, people from Eastern Europe [due to economic migration within the European Union], but there's a lot of people came here in 1990 from the Congo and Angola and lots of people from Bosnia Herzegovina, Croatia and Kosovo who came around the time of the Balkan War. Consequently, there isn't one dominating group, it is quite a mix of people from all over the place. (Local Authority Governor)

The student population is thus drawn from a community which has had and continues to have high levels of poverty, but is one which has changed significantly in terms of ethnicity during the current century. The changes in local population are reflected in the school with not only sharp increases in the ethnic mix, but also with a general rising trend of students who are eligible for free school meals (the most common indicator of poverty in compulsory education). There has also been a notable increase in the proportion of students for whom English is not their first language (see Tables 1.2 and 1.3)

THE FIRST STEPS ON THE SCHOOL JOURNEY TO IMPROVEMENT

We get ahead of ourselves, however, as the school journey to improvement began when the borough was constituted mainly of white working-class families in the period up to the beginning of the current century. By the last decade of the twentieth century, the school reputation and attainment of students had fallen dramatically from its fairly respectable reputation as

Table 1.2 Basic characteristics by national curriculum year group

NC year group	Number on roll	% Boy/girl	% Free school meals[a]	% Minority ethnic group	% 1st language not English	% Special education needs	Children looked after
7	301	48.5/51.15	44.9	59.3	36.9	15.3	3
8	298	50.0/50.0	47.7	45.9	29.2	17.1	3
9	296	51.7/48.3	43.6	44.9	29.3	17.9	2
10	295	54.6/45.4	40.0	38.1	24.5	24.1	0
11	282	55.7/44.3	33.3	33.0	25.3	23.8	1
Post-compulsory	380	50.8/49.2	–	30.8	22.4	23.2	0

Source Ofsted (2013): RAISEonline 2013 summary report
[a]The categorisation of pupils eligible for free school meals (FSM) changed in 2012. Pupils are classed as FSM if they have been eligible for and claiming FSM at any time in the last 6 years

the Robert Clack School to become known locally as the 'Robert Crap' school.

Opinions differ as to how the school had slipped from its previous reputation, but all of those we asked were in no doubt that student attainment on national examinations was typically well below expectations and that misbehaviour was a major factor. One teacher who had witnessed the growing problem of misbehaviour first hand described the corridors and playgrounds of the school as 'no-go areas'.

> … if you were a decent teacher, your own classroom was your enclave and you stayed in it, you didn't go out in corridors, because you would see things you didn't really want to see. [So] you either walked away from it, which was obviously some people's approach, or you had to do something about it, which then caused you massive, massive headaches. Nothing was ever as simple as 'can you stop now'? (Teacher with over 30 years at the school)

Our interview participants who knew the school during the last two decades of the previous century typically recalled two key aspects that contributed to the decline of the school: a lack of focus on student attainment and a lax attitude to student misbehaviour. A wide range of apocryphal stories tell of poor attendance, student unrest, poor discipline and belligerent parental engagement which left teachers generally feeling uneasy and unsupported. Although it was difficult to identify any key statistics that demonstrated the

Table 1.3   Ethnic groups and English as a first language

Ethnic group	School %			National %
	2011	2012	2013	2013
White				
British	69.1	64.3	56.9	72.7
Irish	0.1	0.3	0.2	0.3
Traveller of Irish heritage	0.0	0.0	0.0	0.1
Romany or Gypsy	0.1	0.0	0.0	0.2
Any other white background	4.3	6.5	8.4	4.3
Mixed				
White and Black Caribbean	1.8	2.2	1.9	1.4
White and Black African	0.5	0.6	0.4	0.5
White and Asian	0.2	0.2	0.4	1.0
Any other mixed background	0.9	1.0	1.2	1.6
Asian or Asian British				
Indian	1.1	1.3	1.7	2.6
Pakistani	0.7	1.0	1.7	3.9
Bangladeshi	1.8	2.5	2.7	1.6
Any other Asian background	0.7	1.0	1.2	1.6
Black or Black British				
Caribbean	2.7	2.4	2.5	1.3
African	13.1	13.5	15.3	3.3
Any other Black background	1.8	2.0	2.0	0.6
Chinese	0.1	0.2	0.2	0.4
Any other ethnic group	0.7	0.5	1.0	1.5
Parent/Pupil preferred not to say	0.1	0.0	0.0	0.5
Ethnicity not known	0.3	0.5	2.3	0.4
First language				
English	78.4	76.2	70.1	83.9
Other	21.0	23.3	26.9	16.9
Unclassified	0.5	0.5	3.0	0.2

Source Ofsted (2013): RAISEonline 2013 summary report

school to be any worse than other similar schools in the borough, there appeared to be a common perception within the local community that this was not a school with anything other than a poor and declining reputation. Applications to the school fell to well below their intake capacity, student attendance was low (and at appalling levels in the upper school) and the local perception was apparently fuelled by gossip in the absence of hard data. An interesting aspect of our research was having a number of participants who had both attended the school as a student and were now employed by the school. One key member of the current senior leadership team was such an example and describes his memory as:

> By the time I left the school in 1996 the reputation of this school was rock bottom, I mean, it was terrible, and the school went through its really bad phase in the three years before Paul became headteacher in 1997. (SLT member)

This general view of the school was not entirely shared by the LEA, however, which considered it to be a school in need of improvement, but not the worst in the borough. According to the former Chief Inspector whilst it was true that examination results and local perceptions of the school were low 'it wasn't a school that sort of by their own behaviour or academic terms stood right out from all the others as a crisis institution'. Pockets of excellence could be found in the school, with teachers saying it was possible to be your 'own boss in your own classroom'.

In many ways, this summation could be viewed as an indictment of the state of secondary education in the borough as a whole, with the implication that the Robert Clack School was not the worst of all. Irrespective of such a view the situation was appalling and seemingly getting worse during the early 1990s. As suggested by the former Chief Inspector, there were parts of the school where good quality education could be found, however, with one department consistently having done extremely well in terms of results (and behaviour), so much so that it attracted attention from outside the borough. The operating norms and outcomes from the History department, led by Paul Grant, led to the publication of an academic paper entitled 'A Very Peculiar Department' which highlighted the importance of establishing a good working atmosphere in the classroom (through applying effective discipline) and of establishing 'the right to learn' for all students (Haydn 1998). What this paper suggested was that with the right ethos, discipline and good quality teaching the students were educable.

The New Headteacher

The success of the history department during the 1990s not only attracted the attention of academic enquiry, but also some members of the governing body and officers within the LEA. With the school as a whole not seeming to exhibit the same drive to improvement as some of its departments, particularly History, and the retirement of the serving headteacher in 1997, the search was on for a candidate who could change the fortunes of the school. A shortlist of candidates was drawn up which included, surprisingly, the Head of Humanities, Paul Grant.

The surprise in this regard was that Paul had not held a senior management role in any aspect of his employment in an era when central government was promoting preparation programmes that were intended to ensure that headteachers would be the cornerstone of school improvement. By 1997, the Teacher Training Agency, a non-departmental government body, was introducing the National Professional Qualification for Headship (NPQH) which was to be a guide to school governing bodies and LEAs as to what attributes, skills and expertise they should be looking for in a headteacher. Whilst this was a new qualification that had yet to make an impact nevertheless, it was normal practice at the time for headteacher candidate shortlists to be comprised of applicants who could demonstrate effective whole school leadership expertise. Although examples of promotion from head of department to headteacher had been seen in the independent school sector, it was virtually unheard of in state-maintained comprehensive schools.

Two of the parent governors we interviewed indicated to us that they had considered Paul as a viable candidate prior to advertising the post, however, having invited him to make a presentation to the governing body that explained how his department was getting such outstanding results as compared to other departments. Indeed, once the headteacher post became vacant he was actively encouraged by these governors to apply, despite his own reservations based on a lack of whole school leadership. After taking account of his desire to make a change for the better to the school where he had been employed since 1990 he became one of some 15 applicants, was shortlisted and after due process was appointed as headteacher. We spoke to several members of the selection panel in our research, all of whom indicated they knew they were taking a risk with such an appointment, but who all agreed with the Chief Education Officer of the LEA at the time who is reported as saying *'I think it is a gamble appointing Paul Grant, but I think it's a gamble worth taking' (Teacher member of selection panel)*. It was the chair of the governing body at the time who summed up best why he was appointed:

> Out of all of that the candidates the one that really shone through was Paul. I suppose in a way he had a distinct advantage in that he knew the school very well, so he knew exactly what he would change.

Consequently, Paul took up his new post in May 1997 with the huge challenge of turning round the school's direction of travel.

References

Board of Education. (1943). *White paper: Educational reconstruction*. Cmd. 6458. London: HMSO.

Crosland, S. (1982). *Tony crosland*. London: Cape.

Department of Education and Science. (1965). *Circular 10/65: The organisation of secondary education*. London: HMSO.

Duncan-Andrade, J. (2009). Hope required when growing roses in concrete. *Harvard Educational Review, 79*(2), 1–13.

Haydn, T. (1998). A very peculiar department: A case study in educational success. In R. Guyver & R. Phillips (Eds.), *Preparation for teaching history: Research and practice*. Lancaster: SCHTE.

Holt, M. (1999). Recovering the comprehensive ideal. *Teacher Development, 3*(3), 329–340.

London Borough of Barking and Dagenham (LBBD). (2014). *Guide to school records*. Available at https://www.lbbd.gov.uk/wp-content/uploads/2014/09/School-records.pdf. Accessed 10 January 2017.

London Data Store. (2016). *Borough profile: Barking and Dagenham*. Available at http://londondatastore-upload.s3.amazonaws.com/instant-atlas/borough-profiles/atlas.html. Accessed 11 January 2017.

National Policy Institute. (2013). *London's poverty profile*. London: National Policy Institute.

Ofsted (2009). *Twelve outstanding secondary schools: Excelling against the odds*. London: Ofsted.

Ofsted. (2013). *Inspection report: Robert Clack School*. London: Ofsted.

Palaiologou, I., & Male, T. (2016). Critical hope or principled infidelity? How an urban secondary school in an area of sustained poverty in England continues to improve. *The Urban Review, 48*(4), 560–578.

Pring, R., & Walford, G. (Eds.). (1997). *Affirming the comprehensive ideal*. London: Falmer Press.

Reynolds, G. (2005, September 13). The seductive art of salesmanship. *The Telegraph*. Available at http://www.telegraph.co.uk/culture/tvandradio/3646520/The-seductive-art-of-salesmanship.html. Accessed 8 March 2016.

Sashin, S. (2011, November 9). Becontree Estate saw East end "reborn". *Barking & Dagenham Post*.

Simon, B. (1997). A seismic change: Process and interpretation. In R. Pring & G. Walford (Eds.), *Affirming the comprehensive ideal*. London: Falmer Press.

Syme, S. (2004). *Social determinants of health: The community as an empow-ered partner.* Available from http://www.cdc.gov/pcd/issues/2004/jan/03_0001.htm. Accessed August 2014.

Wraga, W. (1999). Repudiation, reinvention, and educational reform: The com-prehensive high school in historical perspective. *Educational Administration Quarterly, 35*(2), 292–304.

CHAPTER 2

The Improvement Process

Abstract In this chapter, we explore the processes enacted by the newly appointed headteacher and the senior leadership team to regain adult control of the school and to create an effective learning environment. The initial stage of these moves in 1997 is legendary, with some 35% of students (a figure in the hundreds) being excluded until such time as their parents/guardians met with the school to discuss their children's future. This was the largest number of student exclusions ever recorded and was followed up by a huge number of meetings with parents/guardians which were extremely demanding on staff and governors. Eventually only eight students were permanently excluded, with only two more ever being permanently excluded in the following 20 years, a tribute to a desire to serve all children in the community. Adult control of the school was re-established in 1997, however, and sustained through a relentless focus on student behaviour within the classroom, school and in the wider community. The second stage of the improvement process was to enhance teaching to support student learning and ensure their engagement through the development and implementation of the Robert Clack Good Lesson, a requirement that was still evident 20 years later. The pedagogy that evolved is subjected to critical evaluation, with the discussion subsequently moving on to explore how a culture of success that matched both the standard expectations of school outcomes and the comprehensive ideal was established and sustained. Finally, questions are posed as to whether this improvement was a phenomenon or evidence of a continued pattern of achievement that

© The Author(s) 2019   17
T. Male and I. Palaiologou, *Sustaining the Comprehensive Ideal*,
https://doi.org/10.1007/978-3-030-34156-5_2

would allow successive generations of students to be successful in examinations and life to transcend prescripted expectations.

Keywords Adult control · Pedagogy · Change · Praise · Success culture

The Improvement Process Begins

In the previous chapter, we described and analysed how the Robert Clack School descended into a state of inadequate schooling by 1995. In this chapter, we aim to examine how positive change was effected for the school to the point beyond the normal range of school improvement and to a level where the school was consistently judged as outstanding.

Immediately after Paul Grant was appointed to the post of headteacher in May 1997 three things happened. The first was a meeting with governors to explore just how he intended to lead the improvement process; second, he introduced himself to the staff of the school as their headteacher; and thirdly, he took action in a way that shocked the student body and the local community, many of whom were in a state of self-interest that precluded the school from being a meaningful experience for them. In addition, after re-establishing adult control of the school, a democratic working party of all teachers sought to ensure a student's right to learning could be sustained through effective class management, a process that effected by the development of the Robert Clack Good Lesson at a staff conference in October 1997. The 'Good Lesson' was still central to the school's success when we began our research in 2012 and was sustained throughout our time with the school.

Stage 1—Re-establishing Adult Control

The first meeting between governors and newly appointed headteacher set the parameters of anticipated improvement, with an initial heavy emphasis on student discipline that would demonstrate support for the staff which was to be coupled with a desire to promote a sense of achievement amongst the student body. The chair of governors, for example, suggested a need for 'good old fashioned discipline' that made a statement to the local community that the school was changing. In fairness this was not a surprise to

Paul who had presented himself for selection on that basis, as described by one of the parent governors who was part of the selection process;

> He knew the score better than anybody else because he'd been at Robert Clack teaching for about six years, so he knew exactly what was wrong. When he started as head he was on a mission. He would see clearly the way forward, what to do and from Day One nothing was going to stop him.

The day after his appointment he called a meeting of the school workforce to describe to them how the school was going to go forward under his leadership and presented, by many accounts, a clear and inspiring vision of how things were going to change for the better. Many of the responses we had from participants were typified by the comment from a head of department, appointed in 1989, who described it as a 'really rousing speech which energised the whole staff' and in glowing terms by one member of teaching staff first appointed to the school in 1976:

> The first day he held a meeting with the staff which basically empowered us. He promised us faithfully that things were going to improve. That actually felt like, if I have got a problem now something will be done and that kid will be dealt with. You need that in a school, but also staff felt valued.

This promise to the staff was immediately backed up by his first assembly with the students which was 'like the St Valentine's Day massacre', according a senior member of teaching staff from the lower school first appointed in 1990, in which 'students being were asked to leave the hall for different reasons such as no or poor uniform and talking in the assembly. All students knew from that moment on that the situation was going to be very different'. It was a seminal moment for one teacher, appointed in 1996 at the height of the troubles, who considered that they had 'taken back' the school:

> I went into assembly with this horrific Year 8 class and I was told that I had to escort one of them out as "we will not have this type of student in our school, Mr X. Please escort him to my office."

This quickly led to the third immediate response of the new headteacher in his quest to take back adult control which had been evidenced in his first assembly. Exclusion notices were issued to students on an epic scale, a total of 246 in the first two weeks. In terms of interventions, this was dramatic, by any measure, and one that sent shock waves through the student body and local community who were stunned by such a move.

This last move was unheralded and unparalleled in the English state-maintained school system, not least because each such case of exclusion needs investigation and parental engagement before the student is allowed to attend once more. At one stage, according to the new headteacher, 35% of the school intake had been sent home at some stage, but he was working on the basis 'that the other 65% actually maybe thought that was a good thing that was long overdue'. The work associated with this dramatic gesture is legendary, with Paul describing the action as 'being the only way I could get to talk to the parents'. A governor appointed by the LEA described how subsequently marathon sessions of discussions and appeals, sometimes in the evenings or early mornings, were held to accommodate the parents and guardians who often claimed an inability to meet with the school due to various work or social commitments.

The message going to both the student body and the local community was clear, unambiguous and manifested in many ways in addition to fixed-term exclusions. Students were not allowed off site during lunchtimes, for example, a decision that was welcomed by local people and shopkeepers who had been regularly intimidated by groups from the school. The head-teacher and senior staff patrolled the local streets, travelled on local trans-portation services, visited health centres and hospitals where student con-flict was in progress, or had been evident, and went to the homes of recalci-trant students to engage directly with parents and families. Paul described senior leadership and governing body activities at the time as:

> ... following up every one of those incidents. Not just me, but the team because we re-grouped around saving the school; restoring the reputation and gaining trust [...] Every angry phone call, every angry visitation we followed through. So, in the early days I visited people's houses, I'd knock on the door and say 'I believe somebody threw something at your house, can you give me a description'. I'd be on the buses. I'd be in the tower blocks. There would be photographs taken about crimes. I would go to the shops and even though people would initially give me all this invective because I was there, they also started to say 'we'll give you some credit'. Why did I do that? Because everybody else's confidence had been shattered and nobody wanted to do it. Now once I did it, other members of staff followed me. Nobody was going to do it unless the headteacher did that and because the problems were so extreme – we were being overrun by the community.

In the words of the chair of the governing body, 'we were now being led by a headteacher that had a vision and a plan that was very much in line with what the governors expected'. Key to that early vision, he suggested, was 'discipline on the streets', a physical manifestation of adult control that created the sensation that 'in the surrounding area of the Robert Clack school there will be calm'. Although Paul was at the front of this campaign, he was supported by staff who were on the streets after school, on buses and in the local corner shop. Although there was community resistance in the early days of change to this intrusion into their self-constructed social mayhem, there was also evidence of significant levels of support beginning to emerge characterised by comments from local people such as 'You're doing the right thing, whatever you do don't back off'.

The real challenge of effecting such dramatic change, however, is to be willing and able to sustain it in the face of opposition and notoriety. Interventions into local and institutional social norms inevitably create a backlash in terms of personal abuse, salacious publicity and pressure from key power sources to quieten things down. The initial confrontation with some families whose child had been excluded needed personal courage as described by the chair of governors in one example as 'incredibly scary'. In this instance, the expulsion committee decided to meet in the town hall because they had security staff to provide protection from a heated exchange with members of the family who were security staff from a local nightclub. The resolution and determination of the senior leadership team at this stage meant, in the words of another member of the governing body, '[they] more or less lived here [at the school] and occasionally visited their families'.

STAGE 2—CREATING AND SUSTAINING AN EFFECTIVE LEARNING ENVIRONMENT

There were a total of only eight permanent exclusions following the huge number of meetings with the parents/guardians, but the message was very clear to the local community—the school was in the control of adults. One immediate consequence was that with discipline referrals systems in place and fully functioning, teachers were able to teach in a calm manner and felt empowered and willing to engage beyond their own classroom. The former Chief Inspector attributes the success of convincing the teachers to buy into the new era to Paul's willingness to talk to them individually:

One of the things he never avoided laying it out on the line to all of them individually. There's still a lot of resistance, but the main thing that broke down the resistance was the discipline that he imposed and the behaviour that made it possible for them to teach in a calmer mode. They could see immediately that that was what he was going to do.

The tone was thus set for changing the school, with the next stage being to start the process of enhancing the learning environment, starting with defining the 'Robert Clack Good Lesson' which remained at the heart of the school improvement processes. In truth, there is nothing unusual about the lesson plan, for which there are myriad examples to be found in schools across the world. It was simple three-part lesson with an engaging start which recapped previous learning, explored new concepts and checked what had been learnt at the end. Although initially described by Paul as a 'formulaic approach', he qualified his statement by saying '[more importantly] it's a [student] entitlement and it's professional'.

In the early stages, the approach thus was very directive not only to restore the authority of the teacher, but also to re-educate the social skills of the student body. From then on every lesson was to have clear objectives and learning interaction which 'makes sure the teaching is engaging and assessment is rigorous' (SLT member). The template for the good lesson defined classroom behaviour:

> The kids then know the boundaries; they know what is acceptable and what is not acceptable and they will follow that through by and large. When you've got them working for you rather than against you, the results follow, the relationships are a lot better, and that relationship between teachers and students is so important. (Teacher first appointed in 1990)

This approach was not to be a short-term fix, however, but a long-term strategy as recognised by the chair of governors:

> We know we're not going to see dramatic improvements for the next sort of three or four years because those children are already damaged and they are already in the process. All you're going to do is damage limitation for them, but your real first measure of success is going to come in five years' time.

This was a clear signal of a desire to take a long-term view of the improvement process to ensure that the younger children were to be given the opportunity to maximise their potential. Such a move runs contrary to perceived conventional wisdom in terms of leadership behaviour that was associated with turning round a failing school. The challenges this presented and the leadership behaviours that followed will be analysed more fully in Chapter 4, with the discussion here continuing to be the way in which the improvement process was both sustainable and substantial.

The Driving Force for Change

A student's right to learning was fundamental to the philosophy of Paul who, driven by a personal value system rooted in his working-class background, based his approach to education on the notion of critical hope, giving young people the knowledge, skills and opportunity to choose their destiny (Duncan-Andrade 2009—see Chapter 1). He had grown up as a child in another city with a similar environment to that evident in Dagenham when he took over the headship, where full employment had been followed by large-scale unemployment ultimately leading to impoverished social conditions and a history of low education achievement. In his case, the way in which he saw his parents cope with adverse conditions and the responsibility he inherited as the eldest of seven children led him to wish to provide greater support to others in his role as a leader within the community he now served. In his own words:

> I am probably the first working class person of a position of responsibility they've ever seen in their lives. I won't have the door locked, like it's locked most of the time - you can't see the chief constable, you can't see the chief medical officer, but I was going to make sure they could see the head teacher, because that's very important for working class people. (March 2012)

Driven by a sense of social justice, therefore, he sought to develop an environment within the school which recognised the qualities and achievements of the student body beyond the classroom. Students are encouraged to 'aim high, whether you are a boy, girl, black, Asian, working class white, at the bottom or top of the tree' (Teacher, first appointed in the 1980s). Central to this determination was to recognise achievement, particularly in school assemblies which 'are superb and at the heart of us delivering our ethos [with] 95% of time given over to reading out positive referrals, presenting awards, certificates, badges, trophies, medals and to lectures, homilies and talks about how to become great given the students the idea that they've got a place in the world' (SLT member). The core purpose of the school is summed up by a head of year:

> ... the whole ethos is based on giving working class pupils an equal chance. The focus is to instil in them that they have life chances the same as anybody else regardless of where they have been brought up and for them to have that positive feel about themselves.

The route to sustained improvement was more than merely exerting adult control and demanding conformity to a standard lesson plan, therefore, and was based on a sense of belonging and having a right to succeed. Young people, and their success, was as important as academic attainment, starting with the simple premise that no student was going to be penalised for being different. The aim was to establish an environment of positive relationships between adults employed in the school and students, based on mutual respect and 'a belief that you can succeed and you can be as good as anyone else' (SLT member). 'Every child gets the opportunity here' (Teaching Assistant) and 'our common agenda is to equip them with knowledge, skills and, ultimately, grades to be successful adults and to be successful in the wider world' (Head of Year).

CREATING AND SUSTAINING A CULTURE OF SUCCESS

Following the re-establishment of adult control in the school, the emphasis switched to generating the notion of individual success within the student body. This was clearly embedded by the time we started our research as demonstrated with contributions from members of the student council we met in November 2012:

> The school doesn't brand people and so if you're the best academically you're not going to be treated any differently than someone who's maybe gifted in other ways [...] at every opportunity they've motivated me to go forward. (Year 13 male student)

> Even if you're not the best at like the academic side of the school, you will get a chance to shine and they will recognise what you've done. (Year 12 female student)

The consequences of this sustained approach to student achievement were evident in many ways during our research. Headline figures of student attainment in 2014 showed some 80 students with offers of university places (including Russell Group and prestigious overseas institutions), for example, and over 80% of Year 11 students getting the benchmark attainment of five GCSE subjects (including Mathematics and English). Perhaps more importantly academic attainment was universal by this time whereas in 1996 23% of students had left the school without any academic qualification. It is important to stress that these levels of attainment seen in 2014 were not 'equivalent', but actual outcomes on mainstream GCSE examinations. Many schools elsewhere in the country had engaged in 'gaming', for example, whereby vocationally oriented awards were deemed equivalent to a number of GCSEs. Often this could lead to claims of five GCSE equivalence, where a student could be actually leaving school at the age of 16 as barely literate and numerate.

As may be expected there was evidence of 'academic press' (Hallinger 2005) in the school which we defined elsewhere as 'the drive for enhanced levels of student and teacher performance (particularly in regard to outcomes) required by education systems across the world' (Male and Palaiologou 2012: 108). Students were encouraged to study hard for examination success, but it was not the sole driving focus of the school. As already demonstrated, success was celebrated both publicly and more important probably privately, as suggested by a member of SLT, with 'the little conversations you have in the corridor', which he indicated illustrates the behaviour expected of adults working in the school:

> What Paul said 15 years ago is really permeating the school now, this idea that when they do really well, the children, you've really got to reward them, and it can't be an insincere, "Oh well done", you've got to mean it.

Consequently, there was a relentless approach evident to the notion of celebrating success, a process which was designed to develop the students into becoming adults with a good-to-high level of self-esteem. Very little, it seemed, escaped the attention of the school workforce with most events or contributions to society beyond the school being recognised and celebrated. On one of our early visits, for example, we were invited to participate in Albania's national day, a recognition and tribute to the number of students from that country who attended the school having arrived as immigrants in Dagenham. With a growing local multi-cultural population, the school hosted many such national days and thus developed a very cosmopolitan ethos.

In some ways, there was also a desire to engage students beyond the locality which was most evident in sporting activity. A deliberate choice was made in the late 1990s for the school to field boys' rugby rather than football teams, for example, to take part in matches with schools with who the Robert Clack School would not have previously engaged. There was also evidence of wider participation on an individual level, again in sports or activities that not commonly part of the experience of young people from an economically challenged community. We discovered, for example, several students who had been successful in national rowing championships in 2015, a sporting activity most commonly associated with independent schools. Whilst the recognition of success was endemic to the ethos of the school, this was evidence of the desire for students to transcend their local community. There were a multitude of similar type of engagement from public speaking and debating, the performing arts and work experience that provides further evidence of the wish to expose young people to a world beyond the narrow confines of Dagenham.

This is not to say that there were no longer challenging students and that discipline was not a key issue. There was a quiet, but relentless focus on encouraging good behaviour with the school workforce constantly on the alert for emerging issues. The obvious high profile approach to adult control was gradually replaced by mutual respect between students and staff, but no individual or groups of students was allowed to dominate the culture of the school. Members of teaching and support staff were visible at the beginning and end of each school day as well as during lesson changes and break times. Meticulous attention was paid to behaviour and appearance, but often in an unobtrusive and non-confrontational manner. In one memorable incident, for example, we saw an adolescent boy being engaged in conversation about his earring by Sir Paul who had spotted this as he walked us through the school at lesson change time. The discussion was quiet, non-confrontational, conducted in a good-natured way and allowed the student, who was physically taller than the headteacher, to retain his dignity and to have the chance to remove the offending jewellery discreetly. The end result was that standards were maintained through attention to detail, but in a manner that was not suppressive. This was an example of a holistic process by the school workforce of maintaining control that is perhaps best summarised by the observation of a member of the senior leadership team:

I learned in my first few months that with our students you've got to have your foot covering the brake pedal constantly and you've got to learn to push that brake pedal a little bit earlier than you might do in other schools in other areas.

CAN IT BE REPLICATED?

The challenges faced by the school in the mid-1990s when Paul took over as headteacher were challenging in a local authority with a strong history of socialism and one that featured regularly near the bottom of national league tables in terms of student attainment. At the time, the area had unusually high levels of White British working-class people in comparison with other outer London boroughs with only a small enclave of middle class in Barking which, in the view of the former Chief Inspector, resulted in the local population seemingly having implicit values which corresponded to certain expectations, particularly in regard to schooling and leadership behaviours. Leadership expectations of the local community he characterised as an English or Commonwealth model based on a 'nineteenth century public school figure' which was 'fundamentally important to the operation of the school'. Paul, he suggested, 'fits that model precisely, doesn't he? I mean exactly. He's white, he's big, tough, he's got the big bow-wow, he's the sort of person that all the community thinks is a head, or should be a head'. More importantly, he went on to suggest, 'the community underplays itself' and was 'very, very clever at finding out who is genuinely going to be supportive of them'. The end result, he surmised, was that the community:

> [will] find somebody who implicitly says, "No you're not like that all, of course you're not and you know bloody well you're not, you know you're an able lot, you know you've got intelligence and you know you've got all the rest of it and all the rest of it," and they will support that person up to the hilt.

Paul was an exact fit for the local community, it seems, with whom he has subsequently forged a powerful relationship that allows him to effect change. The pedagogy that evolved also met the expectations of the community in that they 'support instructional teaching' and allowed the Robert Clack 'Good Lesson' to be successful in that it was formed of traditional methods, but applied in a 'context in which they will work' (former Chief Inspector). The questions that remain at the end of our research are whether the Robert Clack approach, based on adult control and the 'good lesson' can be replicated and sustained? We asked all of our interviewees the same question in that regard, with the almost universal response being that it would be difficult to follow Paul (see Chapter 4 for succession planning).

Changing Times, Changing Approach?

It would be normal to think that the English proverb, 'cometh the hour, cometh the man' was accurate when assessing the way in which the Robert Clack School made the transition from poor behaviour and underperformance in the mid-1990s to the point where it was identified in 2009 as one of just 12 schools that was exceeding despite its circumstances (Ofsted 2009). At the time, it seemed to be assumed that the school was successful with white working-class young people, with Paul being invited to contribute to national conferences and seminars in 2008–2009 to provide views and experiences of how to succeed with such groups of young people. Paul's offerings to such events were interesting, however, in that he did not draw attention to the ethnicity of the students in the local authority, instead highlighting the impact of a legacy of poverty and inequality which was endemic to the borough by this time.

As noted in the previous chapter, the poverty levels had not changed by the time we conducted our research, with the local authority being ranked amongst the lowest in Greater London for 10 of 21 social indicators. What had changed was the local demographics with dramatic changes to average age and ethnicity which brought in more in line with other London boroughs (see Chapter 1). This led us to conclude:

[although] the ethnicity of the school population was significantly different [...] the school was even more successful. (Palaiologou and Male 2016: 567)

The key way in which the school continued to improve appears, therefore, to lie in the ability to raise the aspirations of the school population and the local community. Support for continued success, we conclude, is an overwhelming desire to confront disadvantage which aligns to the concept of *critical hope* (Duncan-Andrade 2009) that was described in Chapter 1.

Pedagogical Silence?

The pedagogical approach that emerged during the development of the school from 1997 was in many ways a limited model, despite its undoubted success with transforming the achievements and aspirations of the student body and local community. In the view of the former Chief Inspector, the school, under the leadership of Paul, saw behaviour 'as a means of ensuring that learning could happen'. The principal idea behind the behaviour management was to avoid lesson disruption by uncooperative or misbehaving students, with ample evidence of such students being taken out of lessons immediately. The general ethos is best described by two of the teachers:

> [...] bad kids cannot rule a classroom, but you will struggle to find a classroom now where one bad kid rules the roost. Back in the day, the worse kids ruled the whole classroom. If they liked the lesson, the lesson would go on, if they didn't, carnage! (Teacher with 30 years' experience at the school)

> If there are problems in a lesson the pupil is removed and they then become someone else's problem for that time. The Pastoral Team then deals with them and that allows the teacher to be able to do their job. Pupils in class are not constantly having to put up with negative behaviour. They're there to learn and they know that and they know that any bad behaviour won't be tolerated. Teachers then feel a lot, you know, they're happier in their position because they're doing what they're paid to do, they're teaching and they're supported. (Head of department)

There is criticism of a lack of innovative approaches from the former Chief Inspector, however, who considered most headteachers as hardly ever engaging in pedagogy. Instead, he claimed 'what they do is meld existing pedagogies for the absolute maximum, which is what the Robert Clack Good Lesson does'. He explained that the LEA invested a great deal into the use of dialogic talk in a bid to aid working-class children to have self-presentation, the opportunity to think and make a contribution to the lesson. This, he suggested, was largely absent in the Robert Clack School with students being implicitly required to second guess teachers' preferred responses to questions and not allowed silence to allow for formulation of a personal contribution which could take the lesson forward.

Whilst it is a criticism with some substance, it does overlook the ways in which the senior leaders of the school encouraged new developments in curriculum and diversity in definitions of achievement (rather than simple attainment). Our research showed evidence of curriculum innovation being encouraged, such as a proposal to introduce health and social care as a subject and the freedom to allow monitored use of social media to older students. The views of the former Chief Inspector also overlook the culture that has evolved which promotes diversity, allowing students to develop as individuals rather than conform to a model of citizenship which does not respect such rights. Pedagogic innovation may not be an obvious outcome when viewing the improvement process in the school, but this is a minor critique when evaluating the development of student learning and achievement that has emerged from the strategies employed.

CONCLUSION

The combination of sustained discipline and an ethos of success changed the nature of relationships between the school workforce and the student body and encouraged the development of outcomes that were recognised by both the local community and the wider world of education. By 1999 the school was already satisfying the expectations of the national inspection service with a report that was almost unremittingly positive and complimentary. The percentage of lessons where teaching was satisfactory or better had risen from 73 to 95% and was adjudged to be 'good to very good' in 65% of lessons (Ofsted 1999). The school ethos was described as 'excellent' (and the behaviour and attitude to learning of students also evinced praise) with the report noting that the school provided 'a calm and orderly learning environment' (Haydn 2010: 423). It was a simple formula, as described by a member of the senior leadership team, first appointed in 1990:

> If a student is wrong they need to be told, they need to be punished and they need to be encouraged when they get it right. It's really, really simple.

By example and design, therefore, Paul had set the school on the road to sustained improvement, but had been joined on the way by the rest of the school workforce who were encouraged to buy into the new prevailing ethos. What, in terms of demanding good behaviour, was originally a bold intervention through a radical change of expectations became a way of life within a very short period and allowed for the recognition of student success wherever it appeared. The emergent culture was summed up in 2012 by a member of the senior leadership team who had started his teaching career at the school as a probationary teacher just five years before:

> There are high standards and I would call it 'supportive accountability'. Everybody knows as a teacher what's expected of them, they know they're expected to deliver for the pupils and so everybody is accountable for their result. But that is done in a supportive way, it's not ruling with an iron first like fear of somebody walking into your room and seeing what you're doing. So the ethos is incredibly supportive, incredibly high standard of the pupils and of the teaching staff.

The combination of processes allowed the school to improve and, in turn, for the community to transcend itself and recalibrate the aspirations they held for their children.

REFERENCES

Duncan-Andrade, J. (2009). Hope required when growing roses in concrete. *Harvard Educational Review, 79*(2), 1–13.

Hallinger, P. (2005). Instructional leadership and the school principal: A passing fancy that refuses to fade away. *Leadership and Policy in Schools, 4*(3), 221–239.

Haydn, T. (2010). From a very peculiar department to a very successful school: Transference issues arising out of a study of an improving school. *School Leadership and Management, 21*(4), 415–439.

Male, T., & Palaiologou, I. (2012). Learning-centred leadership or pedagogical leadership? An alternative approach to leadership in education contexts. *International Journal of Leadership in Education, 15*(1), 107–118.

Ofsted. (1999). *Inspection report: Robert Clack high school.* London: Ofsted.

Ofsted. (2009). *Twelve outstanding secondary schools: Excelling against the odds.* London: Ofsted.

Palaiologou, I., & Male, T. (2016). Critical hope or principled infidelity? How an urban secondary school in an area of sustained poverty in England continues to improve. *The Urban Review, 48*(4), 560–578.

CHAPTER 3

Being Part of the School Community

Abstract This chapter explores the experience of the three key sets of players who constitute the Robert Clack School community: the school workforce, the students and the local public, each of whom has features that have coalesced over the twenty years into a vibrant and effective learning environment. The scenario begins with the stories of two members of staff, one the deputy headteacher and the other a head of department, both of whom had been students at the school in the 'dark days'. Each had qualified as a teacher, however, and chosen to work at the Robert Clack School. Their contrasting experiences, it is argued, demonstrate the manner in which the school had assimilated the 'comprehensive ideal'. From there, the chapter explores the experiences of the school workforce adapting to both immediate and long term change as they moved from the descent into decline through to asking long-serving members of staff 'why did they stay'? The chapter then moves on to the student body, most of whom were valedictory of the environment in which they found themselves, to the way in which the school worked successfully with parents and the local community. The prevailing ethos that emerged, it is suggested, is the epitome of the comprehensive ideal.

Keywords School workforce · Student body · Parents/community · Change · Pride

FORMER STUDENTS BECOME TEACHERS

The story in this chapter starts with two members of the teaching staff, each of whom had previously been a student at the school during its low period in the mid-1990s. They are two contrasting stories with a similar conclusion of dedication to the school they now serve.

First, we have Russell Taylor, who was deputy headteacher at the school during our research, but who has since succeeded Sir Paul as headteacher; second, we have Kelly Bevan, who did her teacher training at the school and was Head of Business Studies at the time of our investigation. As students at the school, they were at different ends of the spectrum with Russell being amongst the ablest and a member of the top sports teams whilst Kelly had a more chequered career which led to her being seen as problematic and challenging to the teaching staff. Both chose to return as teachers to the same school in which they grew up, although through different routes as a consequence of their life experiences as young adults. By the time we finished our research, we had conducted many conversations with each which demonstrated the high regard they had for the school in its improved mode and their commitment to sustaining continued success.

Russell Taylor, the new headteacher appointed after Sir Paul's retirement, started as a student of the school in 1989 (ironically a year before Paul took up his first teaching post at the school as Head of History) and left to go to university in 1996, by which time the reputation of the school was 'terrible'. Whilst he was quick to point out that his own time in the school was reasonably comfortable, having been in the top set with the best teachers and in the school rugby team, his younger sister and brother were more exposed to the poor behaviour that permeated the school at that time. This, he suggested, partially motivated him to start thinking of a career as a teacher when he submitted an entry to a writing competition in a national newspaper in which he wanted to help 'young people who've grown up in Dagenham facing challenges, facing adversity. I wanted to help those people be successful, because I felt that I'd always received help'. His entry won the prize, gave him a bursary for university and motivated him further to become a teacher, with a view to working in the borough once he qualified. Initially, he had planned to study English at university, but changed to Economics and graduated in 2000. A one-year Postgraduate Certificate in Education qualified him as a teacher with his first post being in a secondary school in a nearby London borough. Although he enjoyed his time in his first teaching post, he determined to come back to the Robert Clack School once he heard there was a vacancy and joined the teaching staff in 2002.

Kelly Bevan, Head of Business Studies, came through the school as a student on a different track and admitted to exhibiting terrible behaviour, especially during Years 7–9 (the first three years of her schooling which took place on the lower school site). In that phase she was 'always in trouble, out of school and being suspended for various reasons', a factor she partially attributed to not being able to make the transition from primary school. There she had been top of her class and considered to be very bright, yet found herself to be a 'very challenging pupil'. Although she considered she turned herself around a little when she made the transition to the upper school site, she still described her behaviour as 'naughty'. By that stage, she was selective in her behaviour with the teachers, choosing where she would be very good and with 'those I didn't care about I would just be outrageous'. Her path through the school continued in the same way until she left in 1997. During her final year, 'my attendance was shocking and in Year 11 I had one-third attendance [and] I underperformed massively'. She also had a major conflict with Paul in his first term as the new headteacher, having 'really cross words with him and saying things I should not have said'.

(continued)

(continued)

His roots run deep in Dagenham with his father's family moving there before the Second World War of 1939–1945 and his mother's family moving there in 1950 when she was just three years of age. Russell's wife was also from the borough and they had met at the school when they were both in the sixth form. As indicated in Chapter 1, the area does not enjoy a good reputation with Russell reporting that 'people who grow up in Dagenham generally believe that they're growing up in an area that most people look down on [...] and for me that was a big part of my determination, my motivation, to come here and help the young people', leading to him coming back to the school because 'the truth is, because I had such good relationships with my teachers in the sixth form I never felt awkward coming back, at all [...] I just came back and fitted in'. In the first ten years of his time as part of the school's workforce, he was promoted four times to become Deputy Headteacher in 2008, by which time he was line managing staff who had taught him as a student.

Somehow she passed five GCSEs and left school to find employment as she wanted to work and to be able to pay her own rent. The job she got was not meaningful to her, however, and although she enjoyed being independent 'I got really, really bored and I just felt that I wasn't being challenged enough'. This took her back to the school to a sympathetic welcome into the sixth form, taking some A levels. Despite her good intentions, her home life was still unstable and 'I used to kind of float in and out of school [and] massively under-achieved at my A levels, but I got enough to get into university'. Her time at university was not without challenge, eventually finishing the degree part-time, having become a mother along the way. Post-university she got a job at the local crown court which she saw as a 'brilliant job, but I started to see many friends that I knew, that were in my classes coming up in the dock for different types of crime like burglary or drugs and it was shocking to me'. This she felt to be wrong as it 'is because of where they come from and their background situations and they've made mistakes'. This was the point where she rang the school and asked if she could be considered for the teacher training that was running at the school, for which she was accepted and began her career as a teacher in the school in 2006.

The stories from Russell and Kelly illustrate the way the school changed to become one that sought to get the best out of students. A review of Russell's school career shows that even in the most impoverished and challenging schools there will always be successful students. This is not to decry the efforts of Russell or his determination to succeed, but it is not uncommon for students in poorly managed schools to still succeed despite the circumstances.

What Kelly's story tells us, however, is that few chances existed for those who either did not conform or were challenging. Where those chances were on offer, it was because of the most talented and dedicated teachers who sought ways in which to adapt learning opportunities to cater for those students who needed the greatest help. It seems clear from her testimony that here was a troubled young person who self-managed poorly and underperformed, yet had immense talent that remained untapped until she returned to the school as a trainee teacher. At the time of our research, she had been promoted several times and, ironically, was now the head of the department where Russell was one of the teachers. In an amusing aside Russell commented that if he failed to provide good enough performance as a teacher Kelly was obliged to report him to her line manager, which was him!

One part of the story that Kelly did not know was the moment when Paul stayed his hand at the last moment from dropping her application to become a trainee teacher into the waste paper bin and decided instead to find out what had happened to this previously challenging pupil. When we quizzed him as to why he chose to do that given the history described above, he replied 'I am too busy to bear grudges'. Kelly picks up the story again to say 'I got a phone call later that day inviting me in and we had a conversation. He said he was so intrigued just to see that I had finished my degree and was here [applying to become a teacher]. Because I suppose I was such a troubled child and he just assumed [...] and he wanted to see, you know, where I'd been and what I'd been up to and luckily, at that time, there was a space for a trainee teacher'.

The stories of Russell and Kelly provide us the launch pad to explore what changes took place in the school and how these affect both the workforce and the student population. Their stories epitomise how the ethos of student support and the maximisation of achievement has transformed both the internal environment of the school and the manner in which student and local community expectations have been transformed.

THE SCHOOL WORKFORCE—ADAPTING TO CHANGE

There is an unusual pattern of tenure to be seen in the school workforce, with many staff staying much longer than average for an urban school. In all, we interviewed six members of the senior leadership team (including the headteacher), 18 teachers, two local authority officers (including the former Chief Inspector, later to become Chief Education Officer), three members of the administrative team and four teaching assistants. It was obvious that some of the interviewees had been selected for us as participants as their length of tenure was frequently greater than the average for the whole workforce. The 18 teachers, for example, had served on average twice the length of time as the rest of the staff (18 years as opposed to nine for the remaining 100 or so). Twelve of those teachers had been employed at the school before Paul became headteacher, and within that group, eight had been at the school longer than Paul (i.e. before he was first appointed a teacher in 1990). The longest serving teacher had been there 37 years when we interviewed him in 2013 and had even been on the interview panel for the headship appointment process which chose Paul. Similarly, the average length of employment for the three teaching assistants was longer at 13 years whilst their 21 other colleagues who had an average of 10 years.

In part, this skewed population was meant to allow us to see a picture of the school from the eyes of people who had experienced the school at its worst and after the beginning of the turnaround strategy of 1997. Whilst the numbers do not seem to add up for teaching assistants, in that 13 years ago was still a long time after the appointment of Paul in 1997, it needs to be borne in mind that all three were parents of children who had gone to the school and they were also people who had lived locally. This qualified them to hold a perception of 'before' and 'after'. Consequently, we were able to research a number of aspects of the changes to the school which allowed for a retrospective view of the school from the 1990s (which, as illustrated in Chapter 1, was nicknamed 'Robert Crap' at the time) and the outstanding school we saw on first arrival in 2012.

The School Descending into Decline

What is not totally apparent in Chapter 1 is that the school enjoyed much of its early existence being held in high regard by the local community. Created as a secondary technical school in the mid-1950s, the first two headteachers steered a course of high expectations and strong discipline and it was only towards the end of the 1980s that things started to change for the worse. Simple things, such as students not clearing away their plates after lunch quickly descended into general student misbehaviour. Several of the people we interviewed suggested the problems began on the lower school site, following some changes to Head of Year positions which proved ineffective, and migrated to the upper school site over succeeding years. It is important to recognise not all aspects of the school were affected with many individual teachers able to maintain good standards of behaviour and engagement of students within the immediate environment where they could exercise their authority, such as within the classroom or department.

Nevertheless, in common areas behaviour was less satisfactory and often confrontational by the mid-1990s, although not all staff were aware of the decline. One teacher, working within one of the larger departments in the school, reflected that only with hindsight did he become aware of how far the school's reputation had fallen since he joined the staff in 1988.

> I was horrified to hear people talking about my school as if it was, not suddenly but over a ten-year period I suppose, that the pendulum had swung. It had swung from an excellent to a really bad reputation. I was horrified by that because I didn't recognise what people were saying about the school. I didn't see it like that, but it occurred to me that in the school you were your own boss in your own classroom. So what was happening in my classroom might not have echoed what was happening in the classroom next door. I wasn't aware of that, or maybe I was, but it was at the back of my head and gradually the penny dropped that the school had, in fact deteriorated over that time.

All the staff we interviewed who had been in post before 1990 illustrated this common theme and allocated the responsibility for decline in the lack of support from senior leaders that was evident when they sought to deal with anti-social behaviour. Typical of the responses was statement from a teacher who started at the school in 1990.

> People start disappearing out of the corridors, disappearing out of meetings, disappearing off the site as quick as they can, not challenging children because they don't think they're going to be backed up by the seniors and senior teams [...] if I did have any issues I was loathe to report them and when I did have an issue with a pupil and reported it to the head of year, I was told 'just stick it in the book'.

It was evident from this group of staff that what was needed was a good culture and the building of the disciplined approach to both behaviour and learning, as illustrated by the same teacher:

> if you haven't got discipline you've got nothing. You can't fight a war without it. You can't teach kids without it. You can't run a bus timetable without discipline. Discipline sounds like a horrible word, it sounds like something being done to you, but it's not, it's just being organised and being consistent. That's what discipline is.

Subsequently, following the appointment of Paul to the headship there was and remains a strict approach to punctuality, attendance and school uniform. Kelly, for example, recounted a story from her time at the upper school about her being asked to leave a lesson (or just leaving, she cannot remember) and being allowed to wander the corridors and even interrupt other lesson without being challenged, a scenario which contrasts completely with contemporary practice where there is immediate intervention. It was evident, even in the early stages of change, there was a great emphasis on behaviour management with the removal of disruptive students from lessons becoming the standard practice, a policy designed to allow teachers to conduct the lesson according to planned learning outcomes which resulted in, according to a head of department:

> Pupils in class are not constantly having to put up with negative behaviour. They're there to learn and they know that and they know that any bad behaviour won't be tolerated. Teachers then feel a lot, you know, they're happier in their position because they're doing what they're paid to do, they're teaching and they're supported. The Pastoral system is a massive reason why we're successful.

Why Did They Stay?

One question that occurred to us about teaching staff, given the circumstances, was 'why did they stay'? What we found as answers varied from an initial need to keep employed (to pay the rent/mortgage or to put food on the table for the family), through dogged determination not to be overrun by the students to a state of belonging and being a member of a thriving community. Of the 18 members of the school workforce, we interviewed the latter was the key issue, with universal agreement that it was the emerging ethos of the school that persuaded them to stay. The turning point was, of course, when it became obvious not only were that staff going to be supported in disciplinary issues, but a new culture was being created, summed up by a teacher who first joined the staff in 1984 (who we interviewed in 2013):

> … you have moments when you say why did I ever do it? But really in 29 years I can't ever say I regret it. […] It just gets in your blood, it is just a special place, it doesn't mean to say you think have I got to get up and do this again? But it is a special place.

In short, it became a school that changed from 'a school where you turned up from 8.45 a.m. till 3 p.m., did your lessons and had your lunch, to a school where you could turn up at 7.00 a.m. and have a managed session in the gym, to staying till 5.00 p.m., having badminton club after school. So many opportunities opened up. And I think the kids and the staff would have called it more of a society, a family, than this is a school where I go to learn and essentially do my GCSEs' (Teacher first appointed in 1976). This, of course, led to staff feeling valued and wanting to commit to the new environment, perhaps best summed up by a senior teacher who had been at the school since 1990:

> It's really important that you enjoy your job and that you feel comfortable and happy coming to your place of work and also that you're contributing to the organisation. So do I like coming to work every day? Yes, I do. Is it a challenge every day? It certainly is. And are there, you know, are there high expectations of us? Yes, there are. Are there demands put on me? Yes, there are. Am I supported? Yes, I am. So there's a requirement that I work hard, and there's a requirement that I do a good job, but that is within a supportive and a structured environment […] I mean what we had to do to start off with was to change the perception of the school, that this was actually a place that was going to offer your child a good education, and that everybody here was going to work to the best of their ability to make sure that the young person got what they should from the education system. So… Paul introduced things like a presentation evening across the whole year group, and the acts that would be performed by the students were very different to the sort of presentations that are made today. But it was all about building and rebuilding a sense of pride in where you came from. […] all elements of achievement are recognised, but underlying all that is that, you know, unless

you come out of here with decent academic qualifications you are going to have your life chances limited.

Changing the Ethos

As illustrated in Chapter 2 the changes enacted by Paul and his senior leadership team were twofold—to regain adult control of the school and to match the comprehensive ideal. The second was the real challenge as it required a recalibration by most members of the school community as to what were to be deemed effective outcomes and to create a sense of pride in the school and the local community. As we saw in Chapter 2, Paul was driven by an ingrained desire to ensure each student had a right to learn and develop as a person and it was this ideal which led to the recognition of achievement across a wide spectrum becoming a critical feature of the school, rather than merely improving student scores on national tests. The transition from a school in trouble to one that as on the mend was characterised by very few staff and student casualties, an unusual outcome in our experience. We have already seen that very small numbers of students were permanently excluded in the initial purge of miscreants and it became apparent that only a small number of staff decided their careers lay elsewhere.

A focus group of governors interviewed in November 2013 talked of the establishment of a new relationship where students were 'surrounded by this culture, this ethos, which is alien to them, and so they either fit in or not'. It is unusual in our experience to have such a combination of governing body and the school workforce sharing such an ethos. In essence, it is just the identification and application of values and principles that are initially made explicit and subsequently shared. The reason it worked as a strategy is because there were very few rules which make it relatively straightforward to do what needs to be done to meet the values and principles. The core value it appeared to us was that no child was going to go through the school and be penalised for being a child, again part of the comprehensive ideal.

The development of a culture of achievement was illustrated earlier in the description of how the school assemblies played a huge role in developing this change of ethos, as did the informal recognition at an individual, although it may have been overemphasised in the early stages following 1997, as described by a teacher first appointed in 1989:

Compared to now, we were celebrating things that probably wouldn't even get a mention now and we were bigging them up, but it was like we were fuelled on adrenaline, felt we'd turned a corner and enjoyed a marvellous collegiate atmosphere with everybody helping each other.

This teacher was a head of department by the time we interviewed him in 2013, well aware of the need for highly prominent schools (which the Robert Clack School had become by then) to keep a close watch on the thing which most external observers seemingly valued, recognising that 'in the modern world you are judged by exam results and I'm guessing with a very high profile head and a school that's quite well known, you have almost to be bulletproof really'. The issue he was illustrating was that despite the value the school community now placed on achievement it still had to exhibit attainment on a better than expected scale. In other words, student scores on national tests, particularly the attainment of five good GCSEs (preferably including the core subject of English, Mathematics and Science) at the end of Key Stage 4, were the benchmark on which the world beyond the immediate school community would use to begin judging the success of the school.

There was a need to look beyond academic qualifications, however, and to develop life skills which would enhance the chances of students finding employment. Previous generations had found employment relatively easy because Dagenham was a huge manufacturing base, with many people going into the Ford Motor Company on assembly lines after leaving school at the age of 16. Similarly, many others had family connections where they could easily find employment. Now, said the teacher organising student work experience (and first employed in 1990), 'you do need the qualifications and skills more so than ever before. Education is more valued by everybody because most of the jobs now are skill based now, with technology being a key factor and I think kids are very aware of that now'.

What became clear from our interviews with teaching staff was a sense of belonging and wanting to say in the adventure that was the improvement and continued success of the Robert Clack School, perhaps best summed up by two long-serving heads of department the first of who said 'I don't want not to be a member of the Robert Clack community', with the second amplifying this sentiment:

This is the sort of school that you're either in it for two minutes or you're in it for the long haul and I think 17 years is a long haul. [...] I think that young people leave this school better for coming to this school and the fact that I'm a part of that is what keeps me going, I think. It seems a bit clichéd, but I don't mean it that way. I do honestly believe the day that I walk into this school and I think, I don't want to be here, that's the day when I'm going to have to go because I could not. That will be like living a lie then.

THE STUDENT BODY

A key factor in the early days of changing the ethos was to establish a positive working relationship with the most influential students in the school, with one masterstroke being the way in which a new uniform was introduced and adopted in the summer months after the appointment of Paul as headteacher in May 1997. This was one of the first major decisions that formed part of a larger strategy to perceive the school to be in higher station than the local community had typically perceived. Although there had been a 'uniform' before, it was for a simple arrangement of clothing that was plain, a required colour, but non-specific; the new uniform was to be the requirement for a blazer displaying the school logo and motto with the intention this was non-negotiable. A senior leader at the time picks up the story:

> One of the first plans that were put into place was to make sure that all of the students went into uniform and there was a lot of discussion amongst staff, so all the people were involved in terms of choosing it. So what we did, and it was genius actually, is that the head got all of the students that were key players, if you like, within Year 11 and Year 10, and got them into his office on an individual basis, and through whatever means, you know, experiences that he'd had with the students and just his relationship with them, he said 'I want you in that blazer next week'. So, for example, we're introducing our blazer next September and now we're in May so he's getting you and then he's saying, 'I would like you wearing that for a week'. And all of the big names in the school start walking round in these ten uniforms that we've got. So, because they're wearing the uniform, everybody else is quite interested in it and by June we had queues of children arriving early to borrow the uniform to wear it. So it was just amazing and of course all of the staff were behind this and you would say 'how fantastic you look' and 'how great' and, you know, and somebody would be looking disappointed next to them because they'd queued up and hadn't got the uniform, and you'd say, well, you know, you'll be able to have it next week. So by the time September came, it was a huge gamble actually, everybody was outside the gates waiting

for these students to appear, and the school turned into a fully uniformed school with blazers, and it was really very clever and, you know, already then there's a great sense of pride.

It makes a great story, but one that is embellished even more by the memories of Paul:

> I picked out what was politely known as the Mafia and I said, 'get out there and win me some hearts and minds'. And these people came back to me through Joe. When Joe walked into the room he blocked out all known light and he was the acceptable face of shall we say closely cropped hair, and he said to me, "I think you'll find the uniform's going to get off the ground, Mr Grant." I said, "Did you have any discussions?" "Yeah, I did, yeah. I think you'd have been proud of me. I was what you would call persuasive."

As we can see the adoption of the new uniform created a 'a great sense of pride' according to the senior teacher who told us the story and that pride was evident in our meetings with students in the school when we asked the question 'what's it like to be a student at Robert Clack School?', to which we received the immediate reply 'privileged' from a young woman in the first year of her A-level studies. The privilege was first identified as fortunate to be in a school where not only was there was immense competition for places where for every three applications there would be only one admission but was also defined by the student body being a major feature in the decision-making process of the school. The two most obvious examples were in the establishment of a school council with over 300 students (comprising elected representatives and volunteers) and the direct engagement of students in the selection of new teaching staff. In this latter respect, students explained to us that applicants to vacant teacher positions were required not only to conduct a trial lesson, but also be subject to interviews by the students. This, we suggested, was a clear example of trust being placed in their capability to make a judgement to which a male student in his last year of study agreed before going on to illustrate the positive relationships held with the staff workforce, particularly teachers:

> Yes, trust definitely comes into it. In terms of the student-teacher relationship, I think it's unique, because there's not a teacher that you can't speak to, obviously about their subject which they're really passionate about, but you know, if you've got a problem with someone or you've got a problem with something, you know, there's sort of, there's a structure to it, but really you

can go up to any member of staff and do things like that, and what they do is they give us a certain amount of freedom to act the way we want, sort of, you know, academically and you know, even down to things like in the playground. They give us as much freedom as they can, but we know that if we do something wrong, they're going to be there and there's going to be consequences.

The school council was a step in the declaration made by Paul in 1997 that 'the school aim for the student to be an active citizen in an international world', an ambition recognised subsequently by showing the students that their views and requests would be taken seriously and acted upon if they were reasonable. The students we spoke not only provided examples such as improvement in toilet cleanliness, changing of the range of drinks in the vending machines and establishing a sixth form common room, but also illustrated higher order tasks such as editing and publishing the school magazine.

Underpinning this student engagement was the expectation that interpersonal skills would be developed, with each student intended to become 'someone who can relate to people, be respectful, have empathy, can communicate and articulate well, is a team player and at the same time can stand on their own feet and who's got pride in their appearance' (Sir Paul in his first interview with us, March 2012). A common litany used in the daily assemblies he indicated was:

> Nobody wants to work with someone who's rude, nobody wants to work with someone who's disrespectful, nobody wants to work with anybody that's not a team player, nobody wants to work with people who use foul language, nobody wants to work with people who are racist or abusive.

It was clear from our meetings with the students that this was common practice and there was strong evidence of not only an evident code of 'mutual respect between the teachers and the pupils, but between the pupils as well' (Year 13 student), but there was an expectation that 'no-one is ever disrespectful or rude to other people' (Year 12 student). 'The teachers are firm, but fair' said the President of the School Council and

> ... they are kind of like your friend in a sense. I know it sounds a little bit clichéd, but I mean this is effectively the truth. You know, you can go up to any teacher and joke around and have fun, but at the same time you know

your place. I think that in certain schools and in other different schools, that relationship doesn't exist in the way that it exists here.

The students were keen to say they felt part of a community and whilst there were a few individuals who did not conform these rarely tended to be influential. One Year 13 student, by that stage the leader of the school debating society (in itself an unusual feature of a state-maintained school in London), illustrated how she had overcome her initial challenging behaviour when joining the school in Year 7 with the help of the staff and the environment they created:

> When I first joined the school I'd just moved to Dagenham so the area was quite unfamiliar to me. I made new friends yet nobody came to Robert Clack from my primary school. I found the transition very, very difficult so I was always one of the kids who were the most troublesome, but I think what this school and the teachers here at every level do, is they don't just sanction you when you make a mistake or you're misbehaving. They explain to you and they look as to why you're acting a certain way. if I went to another school, if the teachers hadn't been bothered to ask why I was behaving in that way, I would have been a completely different person than I am today. Like they massively changed the way I feel about school today.

Again the students referred to the sense of pride they had for school with one Year 12 student describing how appalled she was when attending other schools which were part of an A-level consortium of schools necessary for ensuring adequate curriculum provision, both academic and vocational, across the borough, describing it as very different before going on to say:

> The teachers walk around in jeans and a tee shirt and they have no control over the pupils. The pupils do as they please. I walked into the school and there's pupils having fights with pupils on their phones, there's people like mouthing off to their teachers, and it's just like, I could never imagine that happening in Robert Clack. Like, ever. It's just so different and so like bizarre to see that in a school.

The final words on the ethos of the school as it has become are left to a Year 13 student who was the first to apply to an overseas university and had been supported every step of the way through staff who had been willing to research possibilities with him and to not only provide all necessary transcripts and references, but also to make sure he was making a decision he was comfortable with:

> Every single teacher I've spoken to has tried to talk me out of it and they've tried to talk me back into it. They've gone through all these different scenarios about me enjoying and not enjoying it to make sure that it's definitely the right decision.

CRITICAL FEATURES OF STUDENT ENGAGEMENT

As part of another research project with which we have subsequently been engaged we conducted an extensive literature review form which we were able to determine five critical features for ensuring student engagement:

1. *Frequently solicit student feedback*: The school should gather information consulting the students of their experiences in everyday life in school, such as how they feel about the content and structure of classes and school policies, culture and activities;
2. *Engage students in studying and assessing their school*: Schools should encourage students to ask questions, collect information and listen to their views about what's going right, what could be improved, and how the school could be improved;
3. *Students should be given opportunities to be part of leadership team on decision-making*: In leadership teams, students' present is essential and their views should be respected as with any other team member;
4. *Invite students to any discussion related to their own learning*: Students should be given opportunities to discuss their own progress in parent-teachers meetings, including any disciplinary hearing;
5. *Schools should consider students as stakeholders and partners in their schools*: At leadership level when decisions are made about the school, students should be consulted and offered opportunities to contribute their views on how goals will be met and their expectations.

It seems clear to us that the Robert Clack School was meeting these criteria and that students felt part of a strong community that supported them, whatever their talents or dispositions. Once again this was clear evidence of the school conforming to the comprehensive ideal.

Working with Parents and the Local Community

In the early stages following 1997, both the governing body and the head-teacher were aware of the need to change the relationship between the school workforce and the world outside of the buildings and grounds if desired improvement was to be sustained. It was undoubtedly a challenge, especially with a parental body that was not overly concerned with what happened in school unless, it seemed, their child was being targeted in any way. One of the longer serving teachers described a 'Dagenham' perspective which as either 'didn't particularly care' or 'would want to come up and fight you anyway, for anything'. It could be argued that such attitudes could be considered typical of any working-class community, especially one where previous generations had found employment readily available. The purpose of school becomes blurred in such situations and more focused on it being an obligation for children, rather than an opportunity to move beyond their current social setting. Parental expectations were low, therefore, but underpinned it seem by an aggressive response to any action that affected their child.

> Even if you said 'Johnny, what are you doing?' - that was it. We had so many parents who just thought the school was open house, they could just walk in and attack the head. Many tried and came and attacked me if I spoke to Johnny in the wrong way, drive the car up through the playground, jump out. It was just an open house and that is how far it deteriorated. I used to consider myself to be quite tiny, but a quite hard nasty bloke who had a heart of gold. If I am telling kids off, I am doing it for a great reason, but parents totally disagreed with me, or the ones that bothered.

The community surrounding the school, such as shops and local transport, were not immune from the deteriorating behaviour of the student body who, amongst other things, was not averse to engaging regularly in combat with nearby schools. The main issue, however, was a generic failing by the students to show respect for others beyond the boundaries of the school grounds. The immediate task in 1997 was obvious in that change was needed to the culture outside of the school as well as within. The engagement of parents and local community is essential to the long term success of any school as we have demonstrated in other works we have published (e.g. Male and Palaiologou 2017). Engagement is a larger task than 'involvement' as it seeks to embed aspirations in the parental body and local community that allows them to supersede the current status and perceptions, which may often have been adopted through indolence, and exceed its prescripted expectations.

The process of change began, as has been explained earlier in the book, with the mass temporary exclusions which sent an unavoidable message to students and parents that behaviour within the school grounds and buildings as going to change. This was supplemented by a huge effort by the school workforce to monitor and manage student behaviour beyond the physical confines of the school buildings. Subsequently, this not only led to a change in the public perception of the school, but also changed expectations. By 2009 the school was already recognised nationally as outstanding with a reputation that was built on something more substantial than success with examination results. The local community was displaying confidence in the school as described by a senior teacher, first appointed in 1990:

> It's not necessarily people that have got children, elderly people have start noticing that the children are well behaved. They start noticing that there are staff out at the shops every night. They'll notice that staff like me travel on the buses and they'll know that if they have got a problem, that they'll phone the school and somebody gets back to them and somebody deals with it. So in the end it becomes about confidence, people are confident in the school.

The bigger platform, however, was engagement with businesses and non-profit associations across the city which was manifested mainly as work experience for students in Years 10 and 12. By 2013, this was a sophisticated process being managed by a teacher first appointed in 1990 who oversees the entire range of work experience and a former parent governor now employed by the school to look after off-site learning as well as managing Year 12 work experience. Here he describes the shock he experienced about the insularity of local people when he organised a school trip for Year 8 students some years previously:

> One of the most surprising things for me that I discovered was when I took a group of about 20 kids to London Docklands to HSBC and one girl was looking around awestruck. So I said, jokingly, "Have you not been here before?" She said, "No, never," and that was... I mean, Docklands, what, it's only five miles down the road and I thought, "Surely everybody's been here". So I did a little straw poll right there with the rest of the kids and nine of them had never been out of Dagenham. Couldn't believe it! I just found it shocking. So, five miles out from such an affluent really good area, but never been, and so really sheltered in Dagenham which is a pretty deprived

borough and that's where they're growing up and their families are and they just don't go, they don't move. So that gave me a bit of impetus to start doing more of that and just demonstrating to them, showing them what they can be.

Amongst the multiple initiatives subsequently developed were building relationships with major organisations and societies and inviting successful people, especially former students, to spark ambition. Both these members of staff were keen to emphasise the value of the off-site learning experiences which included commuting as well as the rigour of work practice, with the work experience manager offering the following thoughts:

> The value is that they're getting life skills, they're getting independence, they're getting the experience of what commuting is all about, which is a fact of life in London, a fact of life for any worker of a good quality meaning that many people have to travel to work the job of their dreams or the job that they really want; it's not going to land on their doorstep. So even that commute, that travel experience has a big work experience value in its own right, getting to improve their timekeeping, their punctuality, their attendance and also mixing in with a vast range of different ages, but also taking on real responsibility and getting real work tasks to do at an early age. Because obviously work is an inevitable fact of life for everybody and it's inevitable that's coming their way and it's important that they get some sort of experience about what is going to be the vast majority of their life, probably until the age of 70 now, if the government have their way, making everyone work until they drop dead! So, my thinking is that they really do need life skills, they need to know what it's like to commute, they need to know what it's like to work in a team and they also need to know what it's like to improve their communication skills and general confidence. Because confidence is an important part of the work experience programme.

Concluding Thoughts About the Emergent Ethos

Our conclusions of the ethos generated and sustained at the Robert Clack School was the epitome of the comprehensive ideal as described in Chapter 1 and by Holt (1999: 330):

> First, there is the notion of *inclusiveness*: the idea that education should be accessible, in some significant way, to all pupils regardless of capacity or background. Second, there is the notion of *worthwhileness*: the curriculum has to be of defensible value, so that it enhances the future lives of its students. (Original emphasis)

References

Holt, M. (1999). Recovering the comprehensive ideal. *Teacher Development, 3*(3), 329–340.

Male, T., & Palaiologou, I. (2017). Working with the community, parents and students. In T. Greany & P. Earley (Eds.), *The changing nature of school leadership and education system reform* (pp. 148–157). London: Bloomsbury Press.

CHAPTER 4

Leadership: Theory and Practice

Abstract In Chapters 2 and 3, we described how the Robert Clack School managed the change to success from a previous failing situation through the actions of the headteacher and the senior leadership team, which were fully supported by the governing body. In this chapter, we examine how leadership attitudes and behaviours were not static, but evolved through subsequent years to create, sustain and extend the ethos of the school to make it one of the most successful state-maintained secondary schools in England whilst not losing sight of its core value—to meet the needs of the local community and sustain the comprehensive ideal. We will demonstrate that whilst leadership in this school has been transformational, and ultimately collective, it has not followed a modelised approach to school improvement.

Keywords Situational leadership · Management · Headship · Collective leadership · Succession planning

LEADERSHIP IN ACTION

Leadership theory, originally seen as a subset of management theory, evolved during the last century mainly from the world of business and commerce. The primary focus of the formal leader of any business-oriented organisation was the profit margin, frequently defined in monetary terms.

© The Author(s) 2019
T. Male and I. Palaiologou, *Sustaining the Comprehensive Ideal*,
https://doi.org/10.1007/978-3-030-34156-5_4

Treatment of the workforce corresponded to the twin needs of effectiveness and efficiency, with a growing realisation during the second half of the century that the use of labour was less productive than their involvement and engagement. The general direction of travel in this regard was towards *transformational* rather than *transactional* leadership, with both approaches based on an understanding that leadership involves the ability or capacity to gain results from people through persuasion to achieve a shared purpose (Mir 2010).

Transactional leadership relies on a system of rewards and punishment that work as key motivators, whereas with transformational leadership a common goal is supported by engaging one person with another in a relationship that raises their level of motivation and morality. The key desired outcome in both approaches is to 'motivate, influence, and enable individuals to contribute to the objectives of organisation of which they are members' (House et al. 2004: xxxi). This was in stark contrast to management models evident in the first part of the twentieth century which were based around the efficient deployment of labour, best described in the model of *Scientific Management* (Taylor 1911). As leadership theory evolved, it identified a need for membership and shared decision-making, with the role of the formal leader becoming one of facilitator rather than controller. By the beginning of the current century, transformational leadership was the expected norm within organisations, with the formal leader being the symbolic representation of shared aims and goals.

Educational organisations, and especially state maintained schools, are typically structures which provide service on behalf of larger society, rather than being profit-oriented. Educational organisations are thus concerned more with process than profit, with their primary responsibility being to enhance the life chances of the student body they served. A further feature is that the highly qualified workforce typically found in educational settings tends to exhibit characteristics associated with members of organisations who expect power to be distributed equitably. In other words, they are organisational members who expect to be engaged in strategic decision-making as well as determining their own actions. Despite this it was not until the last quarter of the previous century that leadership theory evolved that was specific to education, initially with the development of *Instructional Leadership*, which emerged from the early work of Edmonds (1979) who began investigating why some urban schools in the USA were outperforming other similar schools. Until then the more general approaches of transactional and transformational leadership were applied to education in much the same way as to other occupations and organisations, with formal leaders being encouraged to engage organisational members as far as it was feasible in the search for improvement. The impact of instructional leadership, based as it was on maintaining a focus on student learning, was felt most keenly by individual school leaders who could thus identify their key purpose and major avenue of influence to be the enhancement of the student learning environment. Further evolution of this mode of leadership took place as we moved into the current century, culminating in the identification of the construct of *Pedagogical Leadership* which we describe as:

> … an extension of ideas pertaining to learner-centred leadership where the key focus of school leaders is on the personalization of education for the benefit of the learner as opposed to the organization or system. Consequently, we consider pedagogical leadership differs from other approaches in that it is more than just supporting teaching and learning. We see it is responsive to the local community as well as to larger society, to be relevant to situation and context and to carry with it an expectation that actions should not be pre-determined. (Male and Palaiologou 2017: 735)

What needs to be recognised in this chapter, therefore, is the need to explore leadership approaches that are relevant to situation and context and allow the Robert Clack School to move towards sustained improvement. The journey began, as detailed in Chapter 1, with a need to turn round the school in a dramatic and directional manner.

Turning Round a Failing School

An examination of the type of leader needed to turn round a failing school suggested that long-term and sustainable impact needed leadership that would 'redesign the school to create the right environment for its teachers and the right school for its community' (Hill et al. 2016). This particular study of 411 academies in England identified five types of leader, each of which had effected change on a failing school. They were categorised as *Accountants, Architects, Philosophers, Soldiers,* and *Surgeons,* with the study concluding that although each effected improvement, Architects outperformed the others as will be illustrated more fully below.

Accountants seek to grow their school out of trouble. With a focus on balancing income with expenditure they seek revenue increases and entrust teachers to obtain resources and enhance the learning environment. As can be seen from Fig. 4.1, however, the research demonstrated that in such instances student attainment did not necessarily improve, even though financial security was frequently achieved with such leadership. *Philosophers*

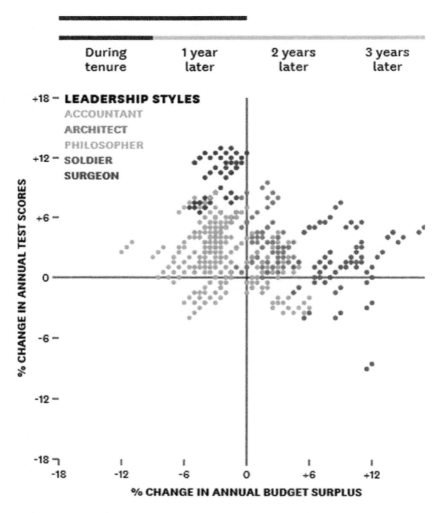

Fig. 4.1   The impact of leadership style

meanwhile seemingly spend their time exploring and debating better ways to establish more effective learning environments without impacting on student behaviour or notions of performativity. The outcome of such a leadership style, suggested the researchers, was no change in student attainment or financial outcomes.

The remaining three styles of leadership did demonstrate positive outcomes in terms of student attainment, but only one—*Architect*—was found to be able to sustain such improvement. *Soldiers* were classified as being task oriented and focused on efficiency, with the elimination of waste as a priority. Their impact was limited to financial outcomes, report the researchers, with the unwanted side effect of reducing staff morale and the aftermath, following their departure, of costs returning to where they were when the school was failing.

Surgeons were characterised as being decisive and incisive, quickly identifying what's not working and redirecting resources to the most pressing problem, most often focusing on how to improve the next batch of exam results. This typically meant a plan of action that removed underperforming or difficult students and introducing a close focus on teaching and learning that would improve results, particularly for those students facing final assessments. Such an interventionist strategy had often been reified in political debate with allusions to 'super heads', as envisaged by Michael Gove when he was Secretary of State for Education in England between 2010 and 2014, being the answer to turning around failing schools (Dejevsky 2013). Their impact was illusory and short term suggested Hill et al. (ibid.), however, with such leaders often departing soon after their arrival. Indeed, many examples of such turnaround leadership of schools by so-called super headteachers have shown short-term gains that required additional efforts to sustain such improvement (Centre for High Performance 2016).

Architects, concluded the research team, are the only leaders who can create and sustain long-term change, through redesigning the school and transforming the community it serves (Hill et al. 2016). Typically, such leaders seek to improve student behaviour, secure revenue streams and improve the student learning environment (primarily through teaching). Furthermore, time and energy should be spent on working with the local community not only to engage support for the changes being made to internal operations within the school, but also to realign expectations. The initial target for improvement in such cases was with the early years of the student experience at the school, a process the researchers determined often means improvement was not immediately apparent, but manifested subsequently.

Defining Headship Behaviour in the School

In the early stages of the Robert Clack School journey to improvement it would be possible to view the actions of Paul, as headteacher, as matching the style of a surgeon as seemingly he was ruthless in his treatment of students who would not conform. Similarly, the close attention to good-quality teaching—the 'Good Lesson'—was a common feature of interventionist headteachers seeking to enhance examination results. The two measures which suggested to us that Paul was not a 'surgeon', however, were the length of tenure of teachers at the school, with many having spent almost their entire careers there and the evidence of investment in the future by working on the younger age groups in the school.

The length of service from the school workforce was explored in the previous chapter, but one further example illustrates why Paul cannot be considered as a 'surgeon'. The deputy headteacher who had been in post at the time when Paul became headteacher was still employed at the school during our research, albeit as the business manager. The fact that he stayed is one typical example uncovered in our research that demonstrated a commitment to developing rather than replacing staff, which is not the operating style of a 'surgeon'.

The other factor we determined about Paul not being a surgeon was the way in which he went about effecting change for the benefit of improving the student learning environment. He and the governors made a plan for long-term improvement which would represent only a small difference to students in the upper school (Years 10 and 11), but a process that would make a major change to the younger age groups, as illustrated in Chapter 2. Thus, Paul was given licence to focus on the longer term, but in fairness to him that was his plan anyway and was something that was within his application and demonstrated in the selection process. The introduction of the 'Good Lesson', therefore, was the first step to create an entitlement to a learning environment that was based on the principle of individual rights. This was fundamental to the philosophy of Paul who, driven by a personal value system rooted in his working-class background, based his approach to education on what we have described in this book as the 'comprehensive ideal'. With such a philosophy underpinning action the leadership style in the school was determined to have a long-term focus and to build the infrastructure necessary to effect sustained excellence. These were not the actions of a 'surgeon'.

Neither could his actions ultimately be aligned to the three other descriptors applied to headteachers by Hill et al. (2016) of *soldier* (seeking order), *accountant* (seeking efficiency) or *philosopher* (seeking to implement an alternative approach to learning). As illustrated above, the most effective long-term change mechanism for a failing school is for the headteacher to be an 'architect' who seeks to 'quietly redesign the school and transform the community it serves' (Hill et al. 2016). The role that Paul played was driven by that long-term purpose, even in the early days of his tenure which was characterised by the fight to regain adult control and enhance the reputation of the school, particularly in the eyes of the local community. Behind that superficial and temporary façade of confrontation, however, was a determination to protect and promote the interests of every student, an approach that was summed up by his statement during his first interview with us in March 2012: 'if these children have been let down that's a disgrace, it's outrageous'. His long-term ambition was to build social capital in an area of sustained poverty and for students to not only transcend their community background, but also for the community to transcend itself.

Formal Leadership in Action at the Robert Clack School

Having considered all the leadership styles offered by Hill et al. (2016) we are of the view that Paul's behaviour blended many the key features, but none of them adequately describes him in action. Instead we have borrowed and adapted the phrase of *Design Engineer* which we consider to be more accurate. A design engineer typically works with others to ensure the product or process functions, performs and is fit for its purpose. In this circumstance, therefore, the ultimate intention was to develop an environment that was based on values and principles, rather than a formulaic approach to improvement.

Such an approach to leadership is beyond what is to be found in high reliability organisations which 'deliver' dependable performance and guaranteed effectiveness (Leithwood et al. 1999) and is more akin with 'Level Five Leadership' which takes an organisation from good levels of performance to greatness through 'a paradoxical combination of personal humility plus professional will' (Collins 2005: 136). Leaders at this level know what they want, but are humble enough to recognise that others in the organisation may have better ideas. Their behaviour is typified by a tendency to give credit to others whilst assigning blame to themselves. As will be seen below and again later, these are behaviour traits that were regularly seen within Paul in his journey as headteacher.

On analysis, there was little in terms of originality to the behaviours adopted as Paul and the senior leadership team initially engaged with the process of developing the learning environment within the school. Indeed, the adopted approach bears a remarkable similarity to the model of leadership developed nearly fifty years ago, initially known as the 'Life Cycle Theory of Leadership' (Hersey and Blanchard 1969). This style was renamed as '*Situational Leadership*' during the mid-1970s and demonstrates how successful leaders could adapt and adjust according to context and circumstances. There was nothing geographical about the 'situation' as it was more to do with the readiness and capability of those other than the formal leader to exhibit behaviours which were at least as productive. This corresponds to the notion that all aspects of formal leadership and management are about influencing others to adapt their behaviour or attitudes, with the essence of effectiveness being the achievement of objectives with and through other people. In other words, formal leaders need to be able to influence other people to take actions they may not have otherwise done if left to their own devices. 'Influence' is a powerful word at this point, especially in the context of a social organisation such as a school, as it implies persuasion, rather than enforcement. The model of situational leadership that emerged from the work of Hersey and Blanchard characterised leadership styles into four categories of behaviour:

- Directive,
- Coaching,
- Supporting,
- Delegating.

These styles were then moderated according to the capability of followers which were defined as their 'maturity' level which were classified on a range of 'low' to 'high'. Each of the four 'M' levels identified indicated the perceived capability of the follower to perform the required tasks ranging from M1 (unable and insecure), M2 (unable, but confident), M3 (capable, but unwilling), through to M4 (very capable and willing). What made the model very successful, however, was the way in which maturity was also linked to expertise and not just experience. In other words, seasoned and experienced staff could struggle with a new task in the same way as a novice worker might in the early days of their employment. The Hersey and Blanchard model was seen as applicable across occupations and to provide a lens through which employee capability could be judged and addressed through a combination of 'sell' and 'tell'. Staff being required to take on a new task could be judged as needing directive behaviour and motivation to change behaviour (high tell/high sell) whereas a worker with growing maturity could achieve the necessary levels of performance where there was low tell/low sell.

The concept of situational leadership can thus be applied to much of the pattern of behaviour exhibited throughout Paul's time in the school as headteacher. In the early days of change when he first took over as head-teacher, he was very much in directive mode and in the habit of instructing others to how to behave. This was very much against his preferred style, which is one of persuasion, but it was an expedient requirement given the situation. As other senior staff and members of the school workforce grew in confidence and capability so he could allow much more opportunity for them to make decisions and take actions that supported the overriding desired ethos for the school. In keeping with the model, however, there were occasions when he felt the need to exert direct authority and to take personal control when circumstances required.

This is a leadership approach which trades on the notion of being visible when things are going wrong, yet invisible when they are working well. This, in turn, lends itself to the notion of collective action whereby all participants are encouraged to consider success as being because of their own actions. The concept of the invisible, but effective leader, is perhaps best captured by Thatchenkery and Sugiyama (2011) who describe such a leader as one who takes responsibility for failure, yet in times of success allows the team to shine and take credit for work they accomplish together. This kind of leadership, they suggest 'finds its roots in cultures with collective mindsets [where] success belongs to the whole and not to one individual' (42). The formal leader 'at this level is thus a facilitator rather than a controller, guiding people rather than directing them [whose behaviour] become less obvious and goes almost unnoticed as colleagues take immediate responsibility for decision-making and leadership activity' (Male 2006: 15). We describe this as building leadership capacity within the organisation and prefer the descriptor of 'collective leadership'.

COLLECTIVE LEADERSHIP

There are many concepts within the leadership theory base which describe the notion of sharing leadership responsibilities and tasks, of which *'Distributed Leadership'* is most commonly used. Distributed leadership commonly refers to a group or network of interacting individuals who engage in concertive action. Such joint action leads to the scenario whereby:

> ... people work together in such a way that they pool their initiative and expertise [and] the outcome is a product or energy which is greater than the sum of their individual actions. (Bennett et al. 2003: 7)

We are reticent to use this construct in favour of 'collective leadership', however, due to two factors: the nature of leadership itself and the relationship dynamic expected within the school workforce. Leadership, as suggested above, is about decision-making, rather than the enactment of such decisions. In other words, leaders make choices about behaviour that needs to be enacted or attitudinal change, whether their own or of someone else. Management, on the other hand, is about the delivery of agreed courses of action. Too often we have seen working situations where we are witnessing distributed management, rather than leadership. Within school settings there is also typically the concept of 'collegiality', whereby qualified teachers expect a level of autonomy especially within their field of specialism. The combination of these two factors leads us to prefer the term 'collective leadership' when describing a preferred mode of operation.

As explored in an earlier work by one of us, any devolution of decision-making comes with a risk and if the formal leader is really looking for decision-making from others within the organisation they must also be prepared to live with the consequences of failure for which, as an individual, they will still be accountable. It is an approach from formal leaders that requires strong nerve as:

> Excellence is never achieved without risk. [When] seeking to enhance the leadership capacity within your school [you have to give] people permission to fail and as Einstein said 'show me someone who hasn't failed and I will show you someone who has learned nothing'. Developing leadership capacity is about individuals learning how to take decisions and actions and that will mean that some mistakes and failures are inevitable. (Male 2006: 102)

It was apparent to us that there was a clear strategy to build leadership capacity within the school and not to rely on the personal capability of Paul as the initiator of change. With the benefit of hindsight, it is possible to see how the shift to operations we witnessed in our research was underwritten, perhaps unwittingly, by the concept of *subsidiarity*. This is the notion of leaving power as close to the action as possible. It is not a new word, but that one that was which seemingly coined by the Roman Catholic Church and turned into a moral principle which drove decision-making. Leadership, as illustrated above, is exercised at the point of deciding what needs to be done when faced with novel or unexpected circumstances. For efficient and effective decision-making, this cannot be a centralised process in any organisation, but the principle of subsidiarity cannot work without mutual confidence between those who are accountable and those who are operating on the periphery of power (Handy 1993).

What we saw in the school was the principle of subsidiarity in action, but this was built on mutual trust which had emerged over a significant period. Staff at the point of action, particularly teachers and student support staff, were shown to be unwilling to engage with issues beyond their immediate sphere of influence in the days before Paul became headteacher. This inaction was evident at the beginning of his tenure as headteacher as we saw in Chapter 1, when the common areas of the schools were dominated by the student body and classrooms often being the only adult safe domain. Before choosing to take personal responsibility, however, staff had to know they could trust their formal leaders to support their actions to change student behaviour and attitudes.

Building trust is a two-way process, however, and takes time as Handy (1993: 125) indicates when he stated that 'a person must remain in post long enough for others to judge the consequences of their actions and decisions [and] to be ruthless if the confidence turns out to be unjustified'. In that instance, Handy is referring to what formal leaders should do if the trust he placed in his colleagues was unjustified. In other words, Paul had to place faith in the school workforce to respond to his change initiative, but be ruthless if they did not respond. In return, the school workforce needed evidence and reassurance that their attempts to discipline the student body would be matched by actions taken by the senior leadership team. Examples of the type of response needed from those with formal leadership have already been provided in Chapter 2, but are summed up by a teacher with over 30 years of experience at the school who described the transition from where the impetus prior to the appointment of Paul as headteacher in 1997 had:

> […] flipped too far, to the liberal side, with the kids having rights, but not responsibilities. Paul brought that back [when he tells the students] 'if a teacher does something wrong you tell me about it, if it is proven, the teacher will be in trouble. If you tell me the teacher has done something and you are lying, you are in trouble. For every right there is a responsibility - if you want your rights, do your responsibilities'. (Head of department—May 2013)

Here we can see the common features of formal leadership behaviours that began to permeate the school—trust and ruthlessness. If someone could not match the trust placed in them, either students or the school workforce, then ruthless action would be taken. As can be evidenced from the feedback we got from participants in our research the early days of directive and ruthless action, particularly when regaining adult control of the school, developed into collective leadership of the school workforce that was underwritten by core values and a determination to embed feelings of success in the student body.

With the sustained concentration on acceptable student behaviour and effective teaching the staff of the school began to place their trust in the formal leaders, the headteacher and senior leadership team. Knowing they would be supported encouraged the school workforce to engage more fully with issues beyond their immediate control. More importantly, however, they began to recognise their voice as being important, their ideas to be encouraged and their decisions to be supported.

This does not mean that there was an absence of conflict, as all organisations based on subsidiarity are 'full of argument and conflict, but it is an argument among trusted friends, united by a common purpose' (Handy 1993: 127). What emerged soon after beginnings of change in 1997, characterised by directive leadership, was a claim of growing trust between the workforce, the senior leadership team and the governing body:

> I do think I've been teaching the team about respect, about empathy, about being strong when it's appropriate and about being sympathetic when it's appropriate. (Sir Paul—July 2013)

In turn, this feeling of trust was transmitted to the community through their own experiences and those of the student body. From those early days emerged the common purpose of seeking and sustaining individual success for all members of the student body, underpinned by a leadership approach which encouraged decision-making amongst the workforce that was relevant to situation and context. The experience of one recently appointed middle leader provided testimony for this:

> Simple things like senior leadership addressing you, asking you how you are, how things are going and actually coming across as approachable […] that you can give an honest opinion and you can get an honest answer. I think those interactions immediately make you feel a lot more motivated to be part of the team and to follow the agenda really.

In summary, therefore, we are arguing that Paul, as the *design engineer*, moved through a range of styles and modes to achieve the declared aim of 'no child being let down'. As a Situational Leader, he chose his leadership style accordingly; as a Level 5 leader, he maintained the ability to exhibit humility; as the formal and accountable leader, he encouraged collective leadership throughout the school community, described by one of the senior leadership team:

> Paul gives his staff a lot of trust and a lot of respect, shows a lot of faith in his team and that filters through all of the layers in the school. In any organisation you've got a hierarchy, but the way we see it is that we have all got our role to play and because of that everyone feels valued. We've got is a system whereby individuals in the organisation are trusted to carry out their responsibilities without too much interference. If you're letting people make decisions they will feel empowered, won't they? If they feel empowered then they feel valued, they take the job seriously and it's highly motivating.

It is a stirring tribute and one, based on evidence accumulated in this research, that is justified. The remaining question is, however, 'was the success of the school based on one man or was it sustainable if he was no longer there'? This became one of our main lines of enquiry as our research progressed and led us to ask frequently about succession planning.

SUCCESSION PLANNING

We talked to range of participants in our research about whether they considered the success of the school was sustainable into the future and, particularly, if Sir Paul was ever to leave his post. It was the topic that frequently cropped up in the conversations we had with Sir Paul, but it was also an issue we pursued with LEA officers, governors, senior leaders and other members of the school workforce. The consensus was that the systems, procedures, processes and people were in place to allow for a smooth transition of headship, but that he was a hard act to follow. It was considered unlikely that the school could once more decline to the point where it was not successfully meeting the needs of the student body and local community, but there were some reservations expressed about the likelihood they would be able to have a new leader with similar levels of energy, expertise and enterprise to make the school outstanding in all respects.

One of the LEA officers serving closely associated with the school characterised the general view when stating that whilst many of the necessary skills had been developed in the leadership team and this was likely to provide sustainability. The conclusion was 'whether you can take somebody of that calibre out of the equation and have no impact, and people not feel it? I don't think that's possible' (LA Officer—May 2013). The previous Chief Inspector of LEA, one of the key people involved in the appointment of Paul as headteacher in 1997, expanded on this view, but highlighted Paul's enthusiasm and dynamism for change to be almost at the level of missionary zeal and located in the school itself:

> His focus has been entirely and exclusively on that place, those people and that particular community. He's simply wanted to make Robert Clack as strong as it possibly can be, but then there's an odd bit a form of quasi-religious element that comes into it which suggests it isn't sustainable. I can't see the school sustaining its position once he goes, although there's just a slight hint with him that he may be good enough, really, really good enough to do everything he can before he goes to stop that happening.

Members of the governing body were of a similar mind, with all those interviewed for this project understanding the prospect of Sir Paul leaving his post was more of a probability than possibility. The timing of those interviews with governors is interesting as the majority took place in late 2013, including one group interview held in November of that year. Paul's influence was central, making him the "marketable brand leader" for the school, according to one of the governors who appointed him to post. If he were to leave (at that time) 'that would send a message into the marketplace that was negative'. The recognition that, inevitably, he would leave one day left the governors concerned as to whether they would be able to find a suitable replacement. Many potential successors, they felt, might be negatively inclined to apply for the position. The chair of governors perhaps best summed it up:

> We probably, I would think, at the moment would not get too many applications for the job. A lot of people would be put off simply by seeing the size of the shoes they have to fill rather than seeing it as the ultimate challenge.

Conversely, the school workforce was adamant that long-term sustainability was more probable, given the way in which senior leaders and other staff had been developed. This, coupled with effective systems and processes, encouraged a general belief that there was 'a really solid team' with 'all the systems in place, everyone knowing what they're doing and the place working like clockwork' (School Workforce interviews—May 2013). Key to the success of that team building was the ethos of the school, as summed up by another head of department with over 30 years of experience at the school:

> [Sir Paul] has done a great job of putting the next strand of leaders in, that are all Robert Clack through and through, and it does need that, and you have got to share the same vision.

This type of feedback mirrors what Paul was aiming for on his 'mission' to provide a rewarding learning environment for the student body and described the challenge as being 'to dig those roots so deep in this type of area that we don't go into the crisis that we had in the past and, therefore, it's a challenge of training a substantial amount of school leaders' (Sir Paul—July 2013). The outcome has been the development of collective leadership, underwritten by core values, for which they feel ownership. It is the epitome of transformational leadership, summed by Sir Paul himself:

> You've seen a hallmark of my leadership is once they pick up my ideas and say it's theirs, we're in business. (Interview—November 2015)

Is the success of the school sustainable? Yes, say the school workforce, 'absolutely it is sustainable if you've got the right people', with one head of department adding 'if it's not sustainable he wouldn't have done his job properly' (interview—May 2013). We close this discussion with two direct quotes from our interviews, the second of which may be prescient:

People have been given opportunities to develop their skills and the aim being that if there is a change at the top the organisation should be strong enough to go on. Provided the person coming in has the same ethos all the people should be in place to keep this ship running and continue on that path to success. (Governor—July 2013)

Paul talks about succession planning and making sure that no one person is bigger than the organisation, that actually the systems are there, are embedded, so that when the person at the top goes someone else can take over and, hopefully, seamlessly carry on the success of the school. The truth is until it happens who knows? (Senior leader—November 2012)

FINAL THOUGHTS

In a previous work by one of us, the analogy of engine oil was used to describe effective headship in operation:

Very few remember the oil in their car engine, yet without it the engine would very quickly seize up. Engines will run for a short time without oil, as will a school without their effective headteacher, but both will grind to halt sooner or later without that subtle influence. (Male 2006: 15)

It is an analogy that works in our view when exploring the leadership practices in the school. Paul's work and the interests of the school often take him away from the immediacy of being highly visible and leaving the day-to-day practices to other senior leaders confident, in the opinion of the former local authority Chief Inspector that 'the school will still be absolutely fine'. The question, however, is will it run as effectively in his complete absence or will it, like the engine described above, grind to a halt without the 'oil' he provides? Most people we interviewed considered he had done enough to leave an effective school that did not need his own brand of high visibility (and invisible touches), although as illustrated above there was a slight concern from the former Chief Inspector that not enough had been done to prepare a successor. That concern seemingly stems from a review of the way in which Paul has undertaken the role of formal leadership, making it very personal and based on incredible levels of energy being expended and doing a 'huge amount of incredibly detailed work on the local community in a way that I don't think I've ever seen any other head do [and putting] himself under massive pressure talking to all staff and laying it out on the line to all of them individually' (former Chief Inspector).

The idea that Sir Paul, as formal leader, spent most of his days talking to people relentlessly reinforcing the key messages about sustaining the comprehensive ideal is one that is recognisable. 'It's the foot slogging', he told us in a personal interview in November 2012, 'talking to everybody every day for 16 years. Not for 16 minutes, not for 16 hours, not for 16 weeks – for 16 years', in other words a process that does not stop:

> Every person I see I don't avert my eyes, I always say hello, I always ask how they are, I always make sure they're fine. And I always make sure I do things in the background. And I say to myself, "You know what? I've got 25 seconds to get from there to there and I'm going to use 24.9 seconds to engage that member of staff because I don't see it as a chore, I just want them to know I appreciate what they're doing. (Personal interview—July 2013)

More importantly, however, he demonstrates listening to be a greater skill because 'in truth I've had a clear view of what I believe works, but, actually, I'm listening all the time to what we can do to improve things' (personal interview—November 2012). Such an approach accords with the quote from philosopher Epictetus (a philosopher who lived in Ancient Greece in the first century A.D.) 'we have two ears and one mouth so that we can listen twice as much as we speak'. The quote is normally interpreted as meaning that you cannot learn much, if anything, whilst you are speaking, but it can also be used to understand that a single vision has to be tested against other people's reality for two reasons: to confirm shared understanding and to check whether there is a better way of reaching desired objectives.

The environment Paul has created is in many ways person dependent, but it has been manifested in such a way that praise permeates the day-to-day existence of all at the school and encourages all to strive for the best. The last word on leadership practice in the school goes to a member of the senior leadership team:

> The way he does it really works, I think, because of this praise and people feel as if they've got to put more in. Very rarely do they get real criticism. If it is there it's specific and it's in a helpful way. He never puts people down. Never. And that's what, it's such a non-negative sort of vibe, that's what people like I think. Combined with everything else, a sense of humour and a pragmatic approach to things.

References

Bennett, N., Wise, C., Woods, P., & Harvey, J. (2003). *Distributed leadership: A review of the literature.* Nottingham: National College for School Leadership.

Centre for High Performance. (2016, March 29). Superheads boost results, but leave the school in chaos. *The Times.*

Collins, J. (2005, July–August). Level 5 leadership: The triumph of humility and fierce resolve. *Harvard Business Review,* 136–146.

Dejevsky, M. (2013, December 7). Super-heads are a super-huge mistake. *The Spectator.* Available at https://www.spectator.co.uk/2013/12/super-heads-will-roll/#. Accessed 1 June 2017.

Edmonds, R. (1979). Effective schools for the urban poor. *Educational Leadership, 37*(1), 15–24.

Handy, C. (1993). *The empty raincoat.* London: BCA.

Hersey, P., & Blanchard, K. (1969). Life cycle theory of leadership. *Training and Development Journal, 23*(5), 26–34.

Hill, A., Mellon, L., Laker, B., & Goddard, J. (2016, October 20). The one type of leader who can turn around a failing school. *Harvard Business Review.* Available at https://hbr.org/2016/10/the-one-type-of-leader-who-can-turn-around-a-failing-school. Accessed 22 November 2016.

House, R., Hanges, P., Javidan, M., Dorfman, P., & Gupta, V. (Eds.). (2004). *Culture, leadership and organizations: The globe study of 62 societies.* London: Sage.

Leithwood, K., Jantzi, D., & Steinbach, R. (1999). *Changing leadership for changing times.* Buckingham: Open University Press.

Male, T. (2006). *Being an effective headteacher.* London: Paul Chapman.

Male, T., & Palaiologou, I. (2017). Pedagogical leadership in action: Two case studies in English schools. *International Journal of Leadership in Education, 20*(6), 733–748.

Mir, A. (2010). Leadership in Islam. *Journal of Leadership Studies, 4*(3), 69–72.

Taylor, F. (1911). *The principles of scientific management.* New York: Harper Brothers.

Thatchenkery, T., & Sugiyama, K. (2011). *Making the invisible visible: Understanding leadership contributions of Asian minorities in the workplace.* New York: Palgrave Macmillan.

CHAPTER 5

A Shock to the System

Abstract Life did not go happily on for the Robert Clack School, however, when an Ofsted inspection in October 2013 rated the quality of teaching and learning only as 'good', which meant the school lost the 'outstanding' title it had enjoyed for many years on with path of continuous improvement. This was a traumatic intervention for the school and especially the senior leadership team who considered the outcome to be a contentious judgement by the inspectors. The decision also appeared to coincide with pressure from central government for there to an academy within the local authority, which gave rise to conspiracy theories. The discussion that follows firstly explores whether the judgement was influenced by the larger political picture of academisation, before discussing the way in which the school reacted and sought to move forward into the future. The school-based data that informs this chapter are drawn not only from the general range of interviews undertaken for this investigation, but also through three additional interviews in March 2016 with the headteacher and the two members of the senior leadership team who were directly involved in the most contentious aspect of the Ofsted judgement.

Keywords Inspection · Academies · Conspiracy · Reflexive leadership · Impact

© The Author(s) 2019
T. Male and I. Palaiologou, *Sustaining the Comprehensive Ideal*,
https://doi.org/10.1007/978-3-030-34156-5_5

School Inspection and the Robert Clack School

Inspection of schools in England has traditionally been conducted by Her Majesty's Inspectorate of Schools, first established in 1839. The role of Inspectors (HMI) was not totally clear for the first 20 years or so as there was difficulty in 'shaking it free from the stranglehold of the Church at a time when there was no clear demand for education from the public' (Dunford 1976: 17). By 1862, however, a revised code of practice was consolidated and by 1870 HMI was deemed to be independent of state and church, a status that still exists. Subsequently, the Office for Standards in Education (Ofsted) was created in 1992 with the intention of establishing a national system of school inspections through a reconstituted HM Inspectorate. The office runs under the direction of Her Majesty's Chief Inspector (HMCI).

Before 2005, each school was inspected for a week every six years with two months' notice to prepare for an inspection. During this period, the Robert Clack School underwent inspections in 1995, resulting in a damning report which is described more fully earlier in this book, and again in 1999 by which time the school was showing rapid improvement. A full inspection in 2004 led to the school being identified as 'outstanding'. In September 2005, a new system of short-notice inspections came into being and under this system the senior leadership of each school were strongly encouraged to complete a Self-Evaluation Form (SEF), which required them to be aware of strengths and areas for development. Inspections generally became two- or three-day visits every three years, with two days' notice and overall on a 4-point scale: 1 (Outstanding), 2 (Good), 3 (Satisfactory) and 4 (Inadequate). It was stated at the time that schools rated Outstanding or Good would probably not be inspected again for five years, whilst schools judged less favourably were inspected more frequently and might receive little or no notice of inspection visits.

Ofsted inspections of the school were undertaken subsequently in 2006 (a limited examination of Physical Education), 2007 and 2011 and for each the outcome was the same—'outstanding'—with the school being identified as one that 'excelled against the odds' (see Chapter 2) and Paul being given a knighthood for his services to education in 2009. National circumstances had changed by this time, however, with the introduction of short-notice inspections, thus removing the time for schools to prepare fully. Figures published in March 2010 showed that revised inspection criteria, introduced in September 2009, had resulted nationally in a reduction from 19 to nine per cent in the number of schools judged to be 'outstanding' and an increase from four to 10 per cent in the number of schools judged to be 'inadequate'. The general election in 2010 and the appointment of a new Conservative-led coalition government later that year saw further changes to the process. The new Secretary of State for Education, Michael Gove, stated in a letter to HMCI that schools would no longer be rated on 'peripheral issues, as we need to refocus inspection on the principal purpose of schools - improving teaching and learning - and dramatically reduce the time and energy spent on other existing bureaucratic duties' (BBC News 2010). Central to the new framework was that the number of areas to be inspected was reduced from seven to four (quality of teaching; leadership; pupils' behaviour and safety; and their achievements).

Changes continued under the new government with a new framework of inspections being introduced from January 2012 and replaced with yet another new framework in September of the same year aimed at putting more weight on teaching and also included changing the 'Satisfactory' category to one of 'Requires Improvement'. From this point, forward schools were judged as possibly needing intervention and support if they were ranked in the third of the four categories and only those that were rated outstanding for teaching and learning would be able to get the highest overall ranking of 'outstanding'.

The Ofsted Inspection of 2013

It is at this point in history that questions started to arise about the independence of Ofsted in relation to the government promoted move to the academisation of schools in England. Figures released in August 2013 show that out of 155 schools inspected since the previous September (which had previously been rated outstanding overall) fewer than a third—44 schools—kept that ranking. Of the others, 91 schools were rated 'good', whilst 20 were told they needed to improve. Two of this last group were given the lowest rating of 'inadequate' (BBC News 2013). The demotion of these schools was countered by the fact that at the same time, 18 of the 24 newly launched Free Schools were graded Good or Outstanding by Ofsted (Department for Education 2013). Free schools were a creation of the Coalition government with the intention of allowing teachers, charities and businesses to set up their own school. Independent of local authorities, these state-funded schools were part of the academisation process and often established to create alternative approaches to curriculum and student attainment. For the Free schools deemed to be 'good' or 'outstanding' within a very short space of time after their inception was an outcome that, to some, smacked of political intrigue.

By October 2013, the Robert Clack School became one of the schools to be downgraded to 'Good', with the only factor not being graded as 'outstanding' being the quality of teaching, with Ofsted reporting:

- Some teaching does not provide sufficient challenge for more able students;
- Not all marking is of a consistently high quality to ensure all students know how to respond and improve their work;
- Teaching observations by leaders are occasionally generous because there is not enough consideration of the progress that different student groups are making (Ofsted 2013: 1).

At the time, it was procedure for inspectors to observe lessons (or at least a part of them) in conjunction with a member of SLT and subsequently grade them (although this requirement has now been removed from the inspection as it is considered to be an inaccurate and subjective process of judging teaching quality). Meanwhile SLT members had already been in the habit of observing lessons and had created a schedule which had been modelled on the Ofsted criteria. Furthermore, they had held regular moderation sessions, often involving external consultants who were trained Ofsted inspectors, to ensure consistency in terms of judgement and subsequent feedback to the observed teacher. It came as a complete shock, therefore, when they found disagreement over the grades that were recorded for some lessons by the inspectors, grades that ultimately were cited as evidence that resulted in the 'good' rather than 'outstanding' judgement of the quality of teaching and learning.

The difference in grades caused a great deal of consternation to two members of the SLT who were directly involved as observers and, in one instance, as the observed teacher whose lesson was graded as 'requires improvement' by the inspector. The observed teacher, a senior member of staff with a reputation amongst his colleagues and students as being an excellent teacher, gave a lesson which was considered by the external inspector as one that 'required improvement', whereas his SLT colleague saw it as an 'outstanding' lesson. As part of moderation sessions with lesson observations held previously with a trained inspector, there had been 95% agreement of the lessons by this SLT observer, leaving him convinced there was 'no void in mine and an inspector's judgment'. He described his experience as follows:

> I had a number of unpleasant experiences during the inspection involving joint lesson observations with the inspectors and me disagreeing with what the inspector actually said. The first one was an observation of a very, very experienced teacher and to make it even more personally uncomfortable for me, this was a teacher who had mentored me, so somebody obviously I know is a very, very good teacher. The lesson he delivered was totally appropriate to the pupils he had - there was learning, evidence of progress and marking, but the inspector was insistent that that was a "requires improvement" lesson with only good behaviour, when in fact it was outstanding behaviour and it was not less than good, by any measure. [...] In some of the conversations I had with the inspectors the judgments that were being made weren't what I would say would be the majority of people's professional opinion about what they saw.

The SLT member in question whose lesson was judged 'requires improvement' had offered himself to be observed to corroborate the view that teaching was outstanding in the school, having been given consistent feedback from LEA staff who were trained Ofsted inspectors that indicated he had a high level of capability. So, in his SLT role he was confident when looking at the teaching schedule on the day to put himself forward for that observation, even though he was heavily involved in the inspection in other ways. In his view, the observed lesson was better than normal:

> I was observed during Period One for about 20 minutes. [...] I knew that what took place during that time was excellent in terms of the engagement from the students, from their response to my questions, from their response to each other's questions and from their response to each other's answers. I knew that it was – I felt very confident.

The reasons provided in feedback from the inspector for this lesson to be graded as 'requires improvement' was that the challenge was too high and had not enabled some of the weaker students to really engage with an abstract concept. Ironically, this was covered during the unobserved second half of the lesson and it was judgements of this type that led to doubt being cast on the capability or motives of the inspection team. Doubts of this kind were reinforced when it subsequently emerged that four of the five-person inspection team were never employed by Ofsted again, either directly or indirectly. This gave rise to several questions as to why a school with secure data of sustained improvement and confidence in the ability to promote student learning and attainment was downgraded for the inspection category of learning and teaching.

What Explains the Ofsted Judgement?

The discussions with the headteachers and SLT raised the spectre of conspiracy, in that there was a political motive driving action against the LEA which had by that stage successfully resisted overtures and instructions by central government to open an academy. Alternative views were that the outcome could be because either the inspection process itself was not 'fit for purpose' or the capability of the inspection team was questionable.

It is interesting to note that the grading of observed lessons is no longer part of the official Ofsted inspection process, so it could be argued that the process itself was not fit for purpose and was too open to subjectivity. This gives rise to the possibility that the inspection of October 2013 was not carried out with due diligence or fairness. As noted above subsequent to the inspection, four members of the inspection team are no longer employed by Ofsted which may indicate that the inspection was flawed. It is equally possible, however, that inspection standards were being applied more rigorously than had been the case previously. The official line from both the Department for Education and Ofsted was that the new inspection framework was intended to be more rigorous than its predecessor. Indeed, the inspectors placed great emphasis on the revised standards at their initial briefing to the teaching staff, so it could be argued that that lessons previously viewed as good or better and outstanding were to be given a lower grade.

The question that filled many conversations with the staff and governors, however, was whether there was a coincidence between the downgrading of the school and the governmental policy of academisation of the national school system? At the time, there was intense pressure on schools generally, and especially within the London Borough of Barking and Dagenham, to convert to academy status. The incoming Conservative-led coalition government of 2010 had accelerated the academisation process that had been a feature of the previous Labour government. Academies are publicly funded state maintained independent schools, established as limited companies, which receive their funding directly from central government rather than through a local authority. By the end of 2009, only 207 schools had become academies, however, a figure that was substantially below government ambitions. The incoming Coalition government appeared to see the conversion of state schools to academies to be a panacea for improvement and subsequently provided the opportunity for large numbers of schools (and the majority of secondary schools) to leave LEA control.

The original purpose of academisation, first introduced by a previous Labour government in 2002, had been to enhance the quality of school provision in areas of endemic underperformance, typically on urban areas of sustained poverty. The process had proved expensive in the first instance as the early academies created before 2006 were funded generously, particularly through the Building Schools for the Future initiative, leading to an initial average cost of £25m per school. There was also an expectation initially that academies would have a sponsor, anticipated to be a business partner, who would provide some start-up and running costs. With businesses infrequently offering themselves as sponsors alternative methods and different funding mechanisms were needed to drive the policy forward. Despite the economic crisis of 2008, which led to government austerity measures, the conversion to academy status was still encouraged after 2010 through allowing any schools rated as 'outstanding' by Ofsted to become Sponsor Academies, with an additional cash allocation of c£100k. Furthermore, the Secretary of State for Education was allowed, under the 2010 Academies Act, to require 'underperforming' state schools to become an academy. Three categories of underperformance were specified, with the most common measure being an Ofsted report of 'requires improvement'. The enactment of that legislation became a key feature with Barking and Dagenham which had sustained a comprehensive system of secondary education and resisted attempts to entice or enforce academisation. Before exploring this position, however, it is germane to look at how the Robert Clack School was aligned in terms of the national drive to school improvement.

With its sustained status of 'outstanding', the school was perfectly situated to take advantage of a range of other government initiatives to place schools at the heart of the drive for sustained improvement. It was already a participant in the highly promoted 'Teach First' scheme, designed to enhance recruitment to the teacher workforce of highly qualified undergraduates, and was bidding to become a Teaching School. The school was also heavily involved in the Prince's Trust which meant it was at the fore-front of the School Direct policy for school-based initial teacher education. In addition to multiple external initiatives with which it was involved, such as education with the Premier Football League, the school was also supplying outreach support for another secondary school in the borough, which had been placed in 'Special Measures'. Indeed, in September 2012, following sustained support from Sir Paul and the temporary transfer of one of his deputies to become acting headteacher, the two governing bodies had agreed in principle for the schools to be joined in a hard federation. This proposal was backed by the LEA and, in an open vote, by over 85 per cent of the parents of the failing school.

The Secretary of State for Education, however, sought to require the failing school to become an academy through new powers available to him, a move that would prevent the planned federation. The initial attempt to enforce academisation was blocked, however, by a court order granted in favour of the local authority. This was the first time that the courts applied a judicial brake to an academy decision, with the judge stating 'the present secretary of state thinks academies are the cat's whiskers - but we know some of them are not' (BBC News 2014). The victory was short-lived, however, with the government being successful on appeal and the failing school officially becoming an academy in 2014 as part an academy trust based in a neighbouring London borough.

This move to enforced academisation was seen by observers and many members of the local community as being an organised strategy against the borough which had long been one of concern for national governments, ostensibly because of perceived underperformance by the student body on national tests. Barking and Dagenham as a local authority, and the individual schools within its border, had resisted the inducements to establish either a sponsored or converter academy, meaning that the government initiative had failed to have the desired impact in this area of London. With the introduction of new legislation that gave power to enforce academy status, however, the government was able to make their desired breakthrough in the local authority. At the time of the Ofsted inspection of October 2013, five maintained secondary schools in Barking and Dagenham had the status of 'outstanding', one of which had been achieved earlier that year. The remaining four all received the announcement that they were to be inspected at the same time in the second week of October. The notice of an inspection given to a school had, by this time, been reduced to half a day with the four schools finding out on the Monday of their working week (October 2013) that they were to be subject to the arrival of the Ofsted team for the inspection on the following day. All four schools were downgraded as a result of the subsequent inspection, with the Robert Clack School being reclassified as 'Good' as a consequence of the grading of the quality of teaching and learning.

The cynicism offered by the local community is not an unreasonable view, for there was no reason to inspect the Robert Clack School at that time. No data existed to suggest there were concerns about the school and there was no adverse publicity or complaints against the school. Sir Paul, speaking in November 2013 and obviously still raw from the experience, told us:

> The data are exceptional, best in the history of the school, and it's far better than the last inspection and monitoring that took place in 2011. The teaching is the best it has ever been.

So the following questions remain—why was it inspected, was the grading process fair and diligent and was it a coincidence that schools in Barking and Dagenham were all downgraded at the same time?

REFLECTIONS FROM THE FRONT LINE

Whilst, and has already been suggested, the notion of conspiracy is an appealing one, it may be more likely the undesired outcome is more to do with the way in which the new framework was interpreted and applied. As illustrated above, the inspectors went to great lengths to highlight the new expectations

> from the first moment of the inspection, not the pre inspection meeting in the morning with the Head and me, but when they went to our staff briefing, the agenda was made very clear to staff because the lead inspector said that the new framework is extremely tough, considerably more rigorous than the old inspection framework, under which we were graded outstanding and we all needed to be fully aware of that. (SLT member, interviewed March 2016)

On that basis, it is hard to conclude that the judgement was harsh or pre-determined. It is more likely that the school was caught out by the new framework, with one of the SLT members recognising that 'if you want to look at something with a certain perspective, with a certain lens, you can find a problem, whether that exists or not'. Some time on from the inspection Sir Paul reflected 'I'm beginning to think more and more it's less conspiracy and more cockup' (personal interview, March 2016). Indeed, that much had been clear in what was, effectively, the debriefing of Sir Paul during his first interview the after the Ofsted visit (November 2013) when he seemed to accept the judgement that 'we need to look again at the teaching, we need to look again at the pedagogy, we need to take the criticisms to heart and we need to get record results next summer'. The emerging intention at that time was to strengthen the senior leadership team and make an appointment at deputy headteacher level to lead teaching and learning.

Likewise, senior leaders subsequently distanced themselves from the shock of downgrading and return to their preferred state of sustained success. Central to their sense of well-being was the lack of reaction by the local community to the Ofsted report with the deputy headteacher reporting 'first choice preferences and total number of preferences have not fallen; we're still by far and away the most popular school in this borough' and headteacher indicating 'there was absolutely no comment whatsoever by any parent about the Ofsted judgement' (both interviews held in March 2016).

WAS THERE LASTING DAMAGE?

There was immediate damage to the sense of self amongst teachers and senior staff, including the seconded deputy headteacher to the local failing secondary school who stated:

> I was devastated. I was absolutely gutted. The pupil outcomes in the type of location that we are in are phenomenal. Unreal! If the Robert Clack school has ended up with a judgment like that we've all had it.

The repair work started the day after the Ofsted judgement was published with Sir Paul delivering a spirited speech to the school workforce which he described as the 'best speech of my life' and, as indicated above beyond the devastation felt from the decision, for most of the school community life quickly returned to normal. The same cannot be said for Sir Paul, however, who felt the 'injustice' of the judgement deeply, describing how it put him in a 'dark corner' for the first month and caused him loss of sleep, because he did not see the judgement coming:

We were on the crest of a wave. The data were exceptional, best in the history of the school and far better than the last inspection. it's impossible for the school to have outstanding behaviour, outstanding leadership without outstanding teaching. (personal interview, November 2013)

Two years later he still talked of 'a burning resentment [...] that a record of excellence over many, many years was undermined and challenged' (personal interview, November 2015). The truth of the matter, he said in his last recorded interview in this study was 'I'll never come to terms with it because it's unjust' (personal interview, March 2016).

Paul was not the only casualty, however, with 'one outstanding colleague ultimately deciding to retire as a consequence', according to a member of SLT interviewed in March, 2016 who also illustrated that 'even a month after the event people were picking bits of metaphorical shrapnel out of themselves'. The judgement also caused the governing body to question whether they had been rigorous enough with the chair reported to be in a state of shock, even when the category of leadership and management was deemed to be 'outstanding', when asking 'have we been challenging enough?'. There were also, of course, knock on effects to the school caused by the downgrading which disqualified them from becoming a 'teaching school', for which there was a financial benefit, but also the chance to grow their own teaching workforce. It was grim situation, but mostly in terms of damage to morale.

This was overcome by a combination of a determination to return to success, an almost total lack of interest in the judgement from the local community and a sense of self-belief exhibited by the school workforce and eloquently captured by the member of SLT whose lesson was deemed 'requires improvement' by the inspectors:

You can't discard what Ofsted say, but for me I genuinely don't care what they say. I care what my colleagues think, I care what the pupils say, I care what the parents say - the main stakeholders. I don't need four or five people to come in for a day and a half once every few years to validate what we're doing.

In many ways that statement seems to capture the spirit of the school motto—*Forti Difficile Nihil* (To the brave nothing is difficult).

References

BBC News. (2010). *Schools inspections slimmed down.* Available at http://www. bbc.co.uk/news/education-11400774. Accessed 1 August 2017.

BBC News. (2013). *Dozens of 'outstanding' schools downgraded.* Available at http://www.bbc.co.uk/news/education-23450685. Accessed 1 August 2017.

BBC News. (2014, January 16). *High Court blocks Chadwell Heath school's academy conversion.* Available at http://www.bbc.com/news/uk-england-london-25752296. Accessed 4 March 2014.

Department for Education. (2013). *Press release: Three-quarters of free schools rated good or outstanding by Ofsted at first inspection.* Available at https://www.gov.uk/government/news/three-quarters-of-free-schools-rated-good-or-outstanding-by-ofsted-at-first-inspection. Accessed 1 August 2017.

Dunford, J. (1976). *Her Majesty's inspectorate of schools in England and Wales 1860–1870* (Durham theses). Durham University. Available at Durham E-Theses Online http://etheses.dur.ac.uk/9794/. Accessed 1 August 2017.

Ofsted. (2013). *Inspection report: Robert Clack school.* London: Ofsted.

CHAPTER 6

The End of an Era

Abstract Life is finite, as was the era of sustained improvement under the leadership of (Sir) Paul Grant at the Robert Clack School. In July 2017, Sir Paul Grant retired from the post as headteacher after 20 years of service in that role. In this final chapter, we evaluate his legacy and the task he leaves behind. Once more the question of sustainability emerges, this time tempered by the news that the headteacher successor is Russell Taylor, the deputy headteacher who began his career towards educational leadership as a former student and freshly qualified teacher of the school. As a young man who grew up in Dagenham and knew the school in its 'dark days', he is well qualified to determine the school's future as he demonstrates in the closing statement of this study.

Keywords Retirement · Legacy · Expectations · Sustained success · Future aspirations

The End of an Era

As may be expected Sir Paul did not stop working after his retirement from headship at the Robert Clack School in the summer of 2017, but moved on to several new positions including one as Education Adviser with the Premier Football League (PFL), a role he describes as being 'responsible for making sure that time out of school for the boys in nine of the clubs in

© The Author(s) 2019
T. Male and I. Palaiologou, *Sustaining the Comprehensive Ideal*,
https://doi.org/10.1007/978-3-030-34156-5_6

the PFL is compensated for, so that they're not missing out'. He has also become an Executive Coach and Professional Skills Mentor in the PFL, a role that involves mentoring coaches in the game—from new starts to elites. He is now a consultant with the University of Coventry and, much to his delight, has been appointed as personal adviser to the Mayor of Liverpool as an education strategist with the aim of effecting similar change in his home city as he achieved at the Robert Clack School. In addition, the Department for Education has retained him as an Expert Adviser for Education, an unusual move with such positions normally being filled by serving headteachers.

His legacy is a state-funded secondary school which is still related to the local authority, one of only 28 per cent in England that have not become academies. More importantly, this is a school which has not only exceeded prescripted expectations, but has also allowed the community to transcend itself. It is now a local society that expects students from the Robert Clack School to go on to greater ventures than might be expected from a London borough which continues to exhibit sustained levels of poverty despite the changing nature of its population. As a tribute to the transition from the mid-1990s where it was at its lowest point to one where students succeeded against the odds let us return to the story of Kelly, the head of department who left the school with a record of under-performance and challenging behaviour only to return a few years later as an applicant to undertake teacher training at the school. In one of the conversations she had with us, she tells the story of what that mean to her and her friends when she was successful:

> When I finally got my qualification as a teacher I phoned my best friend, who was here in the dark days and we've stayed very close ever since, to tell her that I'd got the job and I was going to be working at Robert Clack and then I put the phone down and about 10 minutes later she phoned me back crying and she said, 'I can't believe it, I can't believe that you, my friend, like, have become a teacher'. She couldn't believe that actually someone from our background, our area, was actually... and she says she tells all of her friends. I think that's what's changed in the school for the young people now. It's actually like they believe it, they already think well this is what... Sometimes they go above that, they go like, 'I want to be a doctor' and they want to achieve the very best, whereas before it used to be, 'Oh, don't be silly, you're going to be working over in McDonalds or in Sainsbury's'. My mum's mentality is still, perhaps it was instilled from a young age in an East London family, very much that it's not about education.

She couldn't see me becoming an actual teacher, she had no expectations of me whatsoever. There was just nothing there, there was no 'What do you want to do?' absolutely no expectations whatsoever. Whereas now when they come in at Year 7 the children are told very clearly, 'Whatever you want to achieve, you will achieve if you work hard' and they're told that over and over again. It's not just something that's been said, you've then got all the people working with them to make sure that they do well. They believe it, the parents believe it and so it's like the feedback effect because if everyone's believing they're going to do well and they're working hard, they do well.

The triumph of that transition of the school from inadequate to succeeding against the odds was neither temporary nor transient, however, or the result either of an intervention based on behaviour management (with the school being recognised as a national 'Beacon of Best Practice in Behaviour Management' in a report from the Department for Education 2017) or a focus on what we described earlier in the book as the 'academic press' (the notion of schools pressing for success in standard tests). The school continued to improve in areas of student experience that do not form part of the standard measures, such as those contained within the national inspection framework in place when we carried out our research, with any success being celebrated both publicly and privately. In short, this was a turnaround school that kept improving whilst still sustaining the comprehensive ideal—to provide an effective and successful education for the local student population.

This can be evidenced by student recruitment, with the school having a very small catchment area of just 1.3 square miles. At its lowest point, the school was only attracting just over 100 statements of preference (combined first and second choices) from parents and guardians for 300 available places, whereas it now routinely gets in excess of 900 such preferences each year. The consequence is that admission criteria are now so strict that apart from having a sibling in the school the only other realistic chance of getting admitted is to live in the catchment area. The conclusion to be drawn from this is that the school has not achieved sustained success by recruiting more widely and accepting students from higher socio-economic backgrounds. Instead, it has achieved its success through the actions that have been taken in concert with the local community. In an earlier paper about the school, we argued that this sustained success:

> ... has been through a combination of principled leadership coupled with a determination to provide a success culture for children from challenging

socio-economic circumstances. The school has thus transcended its anticipated station without devaluing the attributes of the local community. A careful balance has been maintained between the demands of the larger society (such as continued examination success) and an unmitigated desire to support the development of students who build on, rather than dispense with, their cultural heritage. This is not the story of school leadership in a white working class community, therefore, but a story of generating educational success irrespective of gender, ethnicity, creed or social status. (Palaiologou and Male 2016: 567)

Neither was this sustained success due to the single efforts of its dynamic leader, but was the consequence of his personal determination to serve the school and community equitably being manifested through a workforce and local community which connected the emergent pedagogy and learning experiences of the students 'to the harsh realities of poor, urban communities' (Duncan-Andrade 2009: 6).

Towards the Future

One question we kept posing to the people we interviewed in our research was whether it was sustainable Sir Paul was to leave the school. Although most of our contributors thought the policies and processes were in place to ensure sustainability, some indicated it would be a hard act to follow. Our view corresponds to the famous statement made in 1972 by Chinese premier Zhou Enlai who, on being asked whether the French Revolution was a success, responded by saying 'it's too early to say'.

Interestingly though his successor is Russell Taylor, the deputy head-teacher, who thus completes a remarkable journey from former student to headteacher in a 15-year teaching career that encompasses two schools and five promotions in his 14 years at the Robert Clack School. For someone who grew up in Dagenham, it is a fitting tribute to the school which has succeeded in sustaining the comprehensive ideal and a challenge he obviously relishes. We leave the last words to him and wish him and the school continued success.

Mohammed Ali, one of my heroes, said, "I don't have to be what you want me to be, I'm free to be who I want to be." Now, obviously he was talking about the slave trade and his slave name as he saw it, but of course, that message is applicable in any context really, you can be who you want. Coming from Dagenham, sometimes people outside of Dagenham will label us as not having much of a chance. So [after listening to the experiences of someone coming from a rough area of London in one of our school assemblies] I finished by saying that we should not allow any preconceived expectations of us to constrain our ambitions for ourselves. That's what I believe in and that's why I believe that we will continue to be successful in this school. (Personal interview—May 2015)

REFERENCES

Department for Education. (2017). *New report with practical advice for teachers on pupil behaviour.* Available at https://www.gov.uk/government/news/new-report-with-practical-advice-for-teachers-on-pupil-behaviour. Accessed 24 September 2019.

Duncan-Andrade, J. (2009). Hope required when growing roses in concrete. *Harvard Educational Review, 79*(2), 1–13.

Palaiologou, I., & Male, T. (2016). Critical hope or principled infidelity? How an urban secondary school in an area of sustained poverty in England continues to improve. *The Urban Review, 48*(4), 560–578.

References

BBC News. (2010). *Schools inspections slimmed down*. Available at http://www.bbc.co.uk/news/education-11400774. Accessed 1 August 2017.

BBC News. (2013). *Dozens of 'outstanding' schools downgraded*. Available at http://www.bbc.co.uk/news/education-23450685. Accessed 1 August 2017.

BBC News. (2014, January 16). *High Court blocks Chadwell Heath school's academy conversion*. Available at http://www.bbc.com/news/uk-england-london-25752296. Accessed 4 March 2014.

Bennett, N., Wise, C., Woods, P., & Harvey, J. (2003). *Distributed leadership: A review of the literature*. Nottingham: National College for School Leadership.

Board of Education. (1943). *White paper: Educational reconstruction*. Cmd. 6458. London: HMSO.

Centre for High Performance. (2016, March 29). Superheads boost results, but leave the school in chaos. *The Times*.

Collins, J. (2005, July–August). Level 5 leadership: The triumph of humility and fierce resolve. *Harvard Business Review*, 136–146.

Crosland, S. (1982). *Tony Crosland*. London: Cape.

Department of Education and Science. (1965). *Circular 10/65: The organisation of secondary education*. London: HMSO.

Department for Education. (2013). *Press release: Three-quarters of free schools rated good or outstanding by Ofsted at first inspection*. Available at https://www.gov.uk/government/news/three-quarters-of-free-schools-rated-good-or-outstanding-by-ofsted-at-first-inspection. Accessed 1 August 2017.

Department for Education. (2017). *New report with practical advice for teachers on pupil behaviour*. Available at https://www.gov.uk/government/news/

new-report-with-practical-advice-for-teachers-on-pupil-behaviour. Accessed 24 September 2019.

Dejevsky, M. (2013, December 7). Super-heads are a super-huge mistake. *The Spectator*. Available at https://www.spectator.co.uk/2013/12/super-heads-will-roll/#. Accessed 1 June 2017.

Duncan-Andrade, J. (2009). Hope required when growing roses in concrete. *Harvard Educational Review, 79*(2), 1–13.

Dunford, J. (1976). *Her majesty's inspectorate of schools in England and Wales 1860–1870* (Durham theses). Durham University. Available at Durham E-Theses Online http://etheses.dur.ac.uk/9794/. Accessed 1 August 2017.

Edmonds, R. (1979). Effective schools for the urban poor. *Educational Leadership, 37*(1), 15–24.

Hallinger, P. (2005). Instructional leadership and the school principal: A passing fancy that refuses to fade away. *Leadership and Policy in Schools, 4*(3), 221–239.

Handy, C. (1993). *The empty raincoat*. London: BCA.

Haydn, T. (2010). From a very peculiar department to a very successful school: Transference issues arising out of a study of an improving school. *School Leadership and Management, 21*(4), 415–439.

Hersey, P., & Blanchard, K. (1969). Life cycle theory of leadership. *Training and Development Journal, 23*(5), 26–34.

Hill, A., Mellon, L., Laker, B., & Goddard, J. (2016, October 20). The one type of leader who can turn around a failing school. *Harvard Business Review*. Available at https://hbr.org/2016/10/the-one-type-of-leader-who-can-turn-around-a-failing-school. Accessed 22 November 2016.

Holt, M. (1999). Recovering the comprehensive ideal. *Teacher Development, 3*(3), 329–340.

House, R., Hanges, P., Javidan, M., Dorfman, P., & Gupta, V. (Eds.). (2004). *Culture, leadership and organizations: The globe study of 62 societies*. London: Sage.

Leithwood, K., Jantzi, D., & Steinbach, R. (1999). *Changing leadership for changing times*. Buckingham: Open University Press.

London Borough of Barking and Dagenham (LBBD). (2014). *Guide to school records*. Available at https://www.lbbd.gov.uk/wp-content/uploads/2014/09/School-records.pdf. Accessed 10 January 2017.

London Data Store. (2016). *Borough profile: Barking and Dagenham*. Available at http://londondatastore-upload.s3.amazonaws.com/instant-atlas/borough-profiles/atlas.html. Accessed 11 January 2017.

Male, T. (2006). *Being an effective headteacher*. London: Paul Chapman.

Male, T., & Palaiologou, I. (2017a). Working with the community, parents and students. In T. Greany & P. Earley (Eds.), *The changing nature of school leadership and education system reform* (pp. 148–157). London: Bloomsbury Press.

Male, T., & Palaiologou, I. (2017b). Pedagogical leadership in action: Two case studies in English schools. *International Journal of Leadership in Education, 20*(6), 733–748.

Mir, A. (2010). Leadership in Islam. *Journal of Leadership Studies, 4*(3), 69–72.

National Policy Institute. (2013). *London's poverty profile.* London: National Policy Institute.

Ofsted. (1999). *Inspection report: Robert Clack high school.* London: Ofsted.

Ofsted. (2009). *Twelve outstanding secondary schools: Excelling against the odds.* London: Ofsted.

Ofsted. (2013). *Inspection report: Robert Clack school.* London: Ofsted.

Palaiologou, I., & Male, T. (2016). Critical hope or principled infidelity? How an urban secondary school in an area of sustained poverty in England continues to improve. *The Urban Review, 48*(4), 560–578.

Pring, R., & Walford, G. (Eds.). (1997). *Affirming the comprehensive ideal.* London: Falmer Press.

Reynolds, G. (2005, September 13). The seductive art of salesmanship. *The Telegraph.* Available at http://www.telegraph.co.uk/culture/tvandradio/3646520/The-seductive-art-of-salesmanship.html. Accessed 8 March 2016.

Sashin, S. (2011, November 9). *Becontree Estate saw East end "reborn". Barking & Dagenham Post.*

Simon, B. (1997). A seismic change: Process and interpretation. In R. Pring & G. Walford (Eds.), *Affirming the comprehensive ideal.* London: Falmer Press.

Syme, S. (2004). *Social determinants of health: The community as an empowered partner.* Available from http://www.cdc.gov/pcd/issues/2004/jan/03_0001.htm. Accessed August 2014.

Taylor, F. (1911). *The principles of scientific management.* New York: Harper Brothers.

Thatchenkery, T., & Sugiyama, K. (2011). *Making the invisible visible: Understanding leadership contributions of Asian minorities in the workplace.* New York: Palgrave Macmillan.

Wraga, W. (1999). Repudiation, reinvention, and educational reform: The comprehensive high school in historical perspective. *Educational Administration Quarterly, 35*(2), 292–304.

INDEX

Printed in Great Britain
by Amazon

82471005R00061